AT LEAST I SURFED

The sun was warm, the water cold. The afternoon light was glistening off the oil slick, low tide, glassy water. So hypnotized was I by the bending light reflecting into my eyes as I stared off into the horizon, that I hardly noticed just how far the rip current has dragged me out to sea. Stuck in this half daydream gaze, somewhere between a dream and reality, life and death, in a trance with a freedom mindset not acquired by the animalistic society ashore. Free from ringing cell phones, and corporate deadlines, and communist gas prices.

 With an anticipation of the forthcoming unfolding, when the elements come together resulting in a reward that cannot be compared to silver and gold, and a feeling that no amount of green paper could buy.

The horizon lines as it grows into shadows of energy. The shuffling of the crowds and the distance behind me restlessly scratching toward me, not to catch the beast but to simply get the hell out of its way. Me however, not paying attention, as I was ripped out by the tides. Somehow placed perfectly, I was in position to flip around and chase this bitch down.

The size can't be measured, was it 6 foot? Or 10? Well overhead that's for sure. A wall bigger than life.... a vertical face caving under my feet as I freefall into the pits as it explodes behind me. The deeper I get, the more time begins to slow until the moment in which it ceases to exist at all. As you start to come to, your perception of time and space is restored. But a feeling remains.

The void in life that every human understands and usually fills by way of money, possessions, and religion ceases to be a burden to your mind, body or soul. What once was a void is now replaced with a filling I can only describe as a dance with God, on his home turf in a fierce and unpredictable playground. When a surfer comes out of a barrel... the adrenaline is still pumping through their heart, arms tingling, eyes focused.

I was completely spit out as the wave gave way to the flats and into the screaming crowd that was cheering me on. I cut off the back and realized that this was a moment I would never forget. Paddling back out to the lineup as the entire crowd of strangers, friends and locals, complemented and congratulated me like I had one a big game of natural energy selection. Nature had thrown me the perfect pitch ....and I hit it out of the park. This was without a doubt the wave of the day.

It's starting to sink in somewhere between the Dolphins and the lineup, the pelicans flying overhead, and the orange sunset. It was the way that I felt at this moment.... the word happiness cannot hold a candle to it. Then it hit me, that thought, "This is what I now live for, this is why I surf."

INTRO

Most people are wrapped up in the financial game in a computer like rat race of society, where the goal it seems, is to spend the first five years your life learning how to walk, talk, and use your imagination, and the rest of it being told to sit down, shut up, and wait in a single column line. This can seem like a very cynical way to look at the world, but they to train you in public schools to accept things the way they are, the way it's taught with no questioning of what life is really all about.

In my opinion the object in this life is to live for the experience of it. Of course try telling that to the 9 to 5 robots in search for the American dream and the infamous Pursuit of Happiness. Happy? What is true happiness? This modern world Society seems to have it all figured out. Or at least, came up with what they think you and I should think it is. In chronological order of what I have experienced and had shoved down my throat it goes a bit like this:

From the moment you are able to grasp concepts, the Western World teaches subculture and their version of happiness. You are given objects called toys such items include a colorful set of plastic keys, a squeaky Hammer, a Nerf gun, and a Tonka truck for the boys. For the girls, its dolls to take care of, and dishes for a tea party. Society is quite the trickster when it gives you these objects. This is because it's to prepare you for the trap that the future has waiting for you once you grow older, in order to make slavery fun.

As a child, you are taught to play such board games with the family as "life" or "monopoly". These games teach you the competition of life, where money is the ultimate Prize. The more money you have, the more things you can do, the more stuff you can buy, the more sense of accomplishment you can gain, so the more satisfaction you can feel. This rewards our competitive nature as humans with paper, as we would reward a pet with a treat.

Now that slavery is fun and you understand the importance of money, it's off to school where you are learned order and taught to read and regurgitate anything you're told. English & mathematics are designed to see how well you can follow rules in grammar in algebraic equations. History is taught in schools to learn about the importance of politicians and the inevitability of War. You have certain useless knowledge crammed down your throat, all while waiting in line, sitting at your desk with your hands folded, mouth shut, taking orders from authoritarian figure whose orders come in a hierarchy. You learn a chain of command from the vice principal to the principal to the superintendent and so on. Kids with too much energy or not enough attention span are dealt with swiftly by being sent to a detention or being drugged up by Ritalin as this is seen as a sickness in the detainment camp for children called Public Schools.

First world education has a narrow-minded establishment criterium made to train zombies for cubicle in a lifetime of robotic repetition. To teach one way to such a diverse crowd, in a place where you have athlete's, nerds, artists, hippies, Freaks, and Geeks, it can be very similarly explained the way Albert Einstein summarized "Everybody is a genius, but if you judge a fish on its ability to climb a tree, it's going to live an entire life thinking it's a moron."

The American dream is what everybody seems to be chasing. The dream says "buy this and you'll be happy", the more you have the happier you'll be, go to school, learn a career trade, stack as much money in the bank as possible before you die and you win. The dream says that if you work hard you'll have a lot and that makes you a winner. Of course if you ask somebody digging a ditch if they're living the dream, the response is one day they will be rich. Most are just chasing a carrot on a stick.

People will play the rat race game out of fear of poverty. This fear, is the same fear instilled in your Primal instincts of fight or flight. The same chemical reaction of not making your rent on time, is the same chemical reaction in your mind has a running from a lion in the grasslands thousands of years ago. The entire system is a play on people's fear. This is not to say that hard work will not get you somewhere but most people get stuck in a loop, running on a rat wheel that never ends until they retire and begin to die, never having truly lived.

In his Infamous line during the inaugural address Franklin D Roosevelt said "The only thing we have to fear, is fear itself." He was trying to remind Americans during the Depression that the nation's common difficulties concerned only material things. To live in fear is a true slavery that you put yourself into willingly. I've had so many jobs I can't even begin to list them. Usually, when I get caught in the loop, I start to look at the people that are in higher positions within the company. I found it very rare to see true happiness. These people woke up every day and went to work all day and then went home and went to sleep and I went back to work and they did nothing else with their life. No passions to be found. Most did this strictly out of fear of losing their job and going into poverty.

Most of the people that I have admired throughout my life, had been poor according to your average first world inhabitant. They have all been artists, musicians, surfers and outcasts of society in various ways. To me, these people were free. To me, these people had it figured out. Because in their mind, they are more free than any CEO Company owner I have ever met. To me they found purpose over slavery.

A lot of people search their entire life for a purpose. Some find it in addictions, some find it in structure, but most find it in religion. Religion can be an extremely loaded word used in the right circumstances. There are so many different types of religions, so many sides of the story, so many arguments about who's right or wrong.
The scientific world has made a laughingstock out of the majority of religions. This is due to their instrumentation and measurements, proving that most of them can be suspect to questioning. No matter what other religions or science gets thrown at faith-based societies, they always just keep faith, and there's nothing wrong with that.

If in modern society, where the majority of the people are poor and will most likely stay that way for life, if a religion is truly the answer, then what makes a religion? There are thousands of types of religions on this planet. Christian, Muslim, Buddhist, Hindu, Rastafarian, and even atheism is a major, and one of the most popular religions today. The foundations of these religions can be found in sacred Scrolls. Some, in histories passed down by Word of Mouth through thousands of years. Most religions are convinced that their religion is the best and don't accept other religions. Each have their own practices and traditions, each have their own Story, and each have their own views of the world.

I believe people look to religion to find peace in their fear of their inevitable death. Others enjoy the fellowship of the religious community. To me, religion, prayer, meditation, and sanctuary are just another way the grasp at the age-old questions of "What does it all mean? Who is God? How do we get closer to him? What is the universe? "

I can't tell you which religion is actually correct, what the universe is, who God is, or a way to see if the concept of what people call God really exists. But what I can tell you is where I feel closest to the universe, God, or mystical experience is in nature.

The ocean is one of the largest forms of nature on Earth. Storms raging in far off places, transfer their energy through wind into the water. The energy travels through the water for thousands of miles until it hits a coastline and eventually collapses within itself in the form of a wave, hits the shore before receding back into the ocean. There is a religious tribe of people around the world that anticipate this Energy's arrival. They wait in God's playground to dance with the universe. They're made fun of by Hollywood and misunderstood by Society. Their history spans thousands of years. They harness the power of these far-off energies like a horse on a chariot. They find peace and solace in the ocean, they are the religion of SURFERS.

CHAPTER 1

I'd be lying if I didn't admit that my journey didn't start because of what I call "The void". It's that thing in your soul that makes you take the leap of faith. Like a bird that outgrows the nest, spreads its wings and finally takes the plunge out into the void. I was living in Huntington Beach where it all began.

I was a truck driver for years because I wanted to travel and get paid for it along the way. After three years over the road and seeing the entire United States from the front seat of a semi, I was ready to get back to the coast where I paid for a nice little apartment about a mile from the beach. My local spot was golden west st in HB.

I worked a schedule of 20 days over the road and 10 days home as a driver. The problem is that when it comes to surfing, it's best to stay in shape. Usually the way to do that is consistent surfing. If you don't go regularly, then your arms become useless for paddling in the water.

You might see surf films and little cuts of guys taking on the wild waves all over the world. But what you don't see is the travel time to get to the places where the waves are, the time and dedication people put into staying in shape both mentally and physically, just to handle the riptides and side currents that can be like rivers washing you down the coast. What you don't see is the paddle out that took an hour, or the cleanup set that broke on them just as they made it to the lineup. You never see the six wipeouts they endured to get the 9 seconds of clip that you checked out on your social media.

When I would spend the 20 days out on the road, I would lose my edge every time. I came home for ten days, and if I was lucky enough to score a decent swell, I was nowhere near in shape to handle it. Not to mention, I had to be sober that whole 20 days out, so when I came home I was paddling uphill with out of shape arms and a hangover from hell to add to my list of self-induced challenges.

By the third year, I had enough. I was ready to work some type of night job driving for the docks so that I could pursue my art of sliding on water with style. Instead of having to get in shape, I decided I was going to stay in shape. If you stay ready, you never have to get ready.

For most people, the work they do and the location they live, defines who they are. They get the house by the ocean, a nice car, a spouse, and they vacation in Hawaii once a year where they never even touch the water, or eat the fish they catch. The house they buy is two blocks from the ocean that they never go to. I've known people that live by the beach because it's "The place to be." They lived there for ten years and I'll visit. When I show up, they go to the beach with me for the "first time in years."

It makes me sick because the location they are paying for, to live by my favorite playground, that they never see, just because it's the "place to be", yet they don't even care to enjoy it. This makes the rent insanely high. So I had to make ends meet by finding something with a surf schedule.

The perfect surf schedule involves having the morning off. The best time to surf in Southern California is when there's no wind, usually in the AM, called "The morning glass." The second that wind gets on the water, the waves "Crap out" or get crumbly. Most jobs work early in the AM. So I had to take a different approach.

I landed a job delivering janitorial supplies in Costa Mesa. It actually wasn't a bad gig and the schedule was a night job...perfect for me. 2pm to 10pm. I could catch the morning glass and even get a nap in before work, and come home at night in time to crash out at a decent hour to start the whole thing over the next day.

I surfed every day like this. I got my weekends to chase girls and party, then surfed all week. I made a decent wage and was able to afford my spot by the beach. This was when I believed I had the perfect life. At 27 I was surfing every day, making money, plus had the energy to stay in shape and take on the surf daily. It was perfect.

Of course, once life sees you got it all figured out, it seems like instead of just letting you be, it usually decides to throw you a curveball. Once you obtain your dream life, life will give you a different dream to chase.

The more I surfed, the more I began to feel different. The more I was in the water and away from people working 9 to 5 jobs, or watching their favorite sports or television shows, the more distant I began to feel from "society." This happened to coincide with feeling something that I didn't see in most people's eyes, happy.

It didn't take long before I was uninterested in normal things anymore. I worked through most sports that people watched, I never had time for shows, and didn't even think about politics, the news or world events. My world was in the water and then time to rest in between that. I wasn't mad at the president, or worried about the Middle East anymore, after all, they didn't even surf ...so why bother.

I didn't have time to even think about that stuff anymore. My mind was consumed by reading weather maps over the gulf of Alaska, or cyclones off the top of New Zealand. All I thought about was high pressure systems that would push the wind offshore so I might get a chance to get a decent barrel.

I noticed that when I wasn't thinking about the normal television stuff or video games but focusing on the weather instead, I could almost walk outside and feel the air and tell you what the weather would be like in the next few days. I could feel the rain coming, or the Santa Ana winds about to blow. I thought I was going crazy. But as it turns out, this is actually how we were for all of history before the last hundred years.

Is it our own search for entertainment or pleasure that missguided us? Did we become so enveloped in distracting ourselves that we've forgotten who we are? What was I discovering that I didn't seem to find in anyone else that was in my immediate life?

As I did my research, I began to read about nomadic people that were away from society so long that they had tapped into some primal instincts that we seem to be ignored in city life. What were we lacking that caused us to numb our "sixth sense" for lack of a better term.

There was a study on pigs that interested me the most. As it turns out, if you take a pink little farm pig that is usually lazy, fat, and docile, and you introduce it to the wild, it will begin to change its look and instinctual behavior within weeks. After a short time in nature, it will begin to turn black, grow tusks, and buck up to people and other animals.

Was I growing tusks so to speak? Was all this time away from distractions bringing me back to some primordial aspect that we have long forgotten? How long was it that a wolf turned into a Chihuahua, how many generations did it take? How long would it take for him to turn back? Maybe just an activated gene? The call of the wild? Why was it that surfing was what brought this out in me in a couple short years?

These are the questions that I would ask myself as I began to evolve more inwardly and began to be a bit of an outcast mentally and spiritually to all the peers I surround myself with. The better I got at surfing, and the more connected I got with nature and the elements, the more I had begun to almost control my own reality. For a hot minute I thought I was going crazy. Or maybe I was going sane in an insane world for the very first time.

Unfortunately when you go through something like this, most people go through it alone. It's a few and far between phenomena. In fact, most people that would go through some type of awakening like this usually do it because they're alone.

The ability to be alone and be comfortable with it, is a unique gift as a human being. In society, if they want to punish a person, they take them away from other human beings. When you get locked up in prison away from society, if they want to punish you even more, they put you in "the hole." This is where they take you away from humans entirely as a form of punishment.

I think during a spiritual awakening, becoming tapped in, or whatever it was I was going through, being alone is the key to it all. There is no mentor, there is no book for it or instructions. First you feel like you're going completely insane, and then it feels like everybody else is stuck in a maze that you had escaped. When this happens, it happens only individually, and it happens alone. Most of the people that it happens to are alone and usually seek out solitude after it's done because there is no more fitting in with the regular daily minutia of life. In religions, a priest is usually ordained. There's usually some type of schooling that goes on where you have a teacher, a promotion, or test to pass. In indigenous cultures, there is something called a shaman. The way he obtains this title is by going off into nature alone for years at a time. By doing this he becomes completely enveloped into the elements.

For me, I knew I wasn't actually crazy. In fact, the way you tell if you're crazy or not, is if you think you're going crazy, that is the first symptom of not being crazy. However, if somebody is being crazy, and they think that they are perfectly normal and that everyone else is crazy, that is the first symptom of an actual crazy person. So by that narrative, just the fact that I thought I was going crazy was the first symptom of me not being crazy which was a conundrum in my mind.

But I knew something had to give, I couldn't keep doing what I was doing in this "dream life". If I felt this way, there has to be other people that feel the exact same way. But where were they? And were they seeking me as well? Do they have the answers that I don't even have questions to yet?

But while I'm seeking out others that may feel the same way as I do, so to speak "tapped in " To a flow state, I had to do more research to figure out what it was about surfing that took me to the edge of that reality. Was there other sports, lifestyles, drugs even, that could help with this process? What was it that was in surfing that caused the glitch in the matrix of my reality?

One thought was maybe it was solitude. In the ocean, you were pretty much on your own the entire time. Even in a crowded lineup, if you have a bad wipe out, you have to get yourself out of there. If you get caught inside, you have to get yourself back to the outside. If you get caught by a clean upset, it's you and just you that is going for a ride. So being alone is a big part of your journey in surfing, and as it bleeds into your land life, you will become an outcast.... simply for being comfortable with solitude.

To be honest, it began to feel like a religious experience in itself. I grew up in a Christian household. In fact sometimes the only book I was allowed to read was the Bible. My father was quite the history buff and used to only let me watch the history channel and read the Bible. So I was definitely well-versed in religious experiences. I used to go to all the youth group rallies and I would cry and sing and pray. At the time I had no other experience in life. To me singing a song for the Lord was the most divine experience one could have. But I was also told that. I felt like when I was part of the church, I was told how to feel. It was an experience that I just lived through other people's illusions. To this day my religious words of wisdom are "I don't know."

But whatever was happening to me felt in itself like a religious experience. I needed to seek out a priest, a wise man, somebody who has gone through this that is meditating on a hill ...in a loincloth somewhere that can explain what is going on ....and point me in the right direction.

In my early days of surfing, there was a guy down the street named Kelley (not Slater) that was a surfer that would give me rides to the beach. He would teach me about where the waves came from and why. "North swells in the winter from Alaska, south swells in the summer from Antarctica." He would educate me about weather patterns and what to look for. We used to get up early in the morning before the sun came up or the beaches were open, we would jump the fence at Bolsa Chica State Beach before it was open and Surf alone as the sun would rise, and about the time people started paddling to the line- up, we were already surfed out.

I would go as far as to say that he was my mentor when it came to the "Way of the Surfer." He was more like a California kid prankster than a Japanese sensei and we always had a good time, but he taught me more things than anybody else. He would take me to surf locations up and down the coast and teach me about them. He would say something that only made sense when I began to make surfing my entire life.... "Only a surfer knows the feeling!"

In the surfing world this was a common saying that I had no idea existed at the time or why. But as I began to integrate into the sport and make it my lifestyle, it was the only thing that made sense. Surfing has the ability to make family out of friends because you have each other's back in the water, and you go through hell sometimes together, just to get some good waves. I lost touch with Kelley after he moved from California, but he was always more than a brother to me because of the waves we got, and the times we had in the water that I will never have anybody else. How was it that you could be close to somebody like that through experiences? The way soldiers must've felt after war and having each other's back is the only way I can explain it.

At this point I had too many questions and not enough answers. So I began to travel a bit and search for answers.

CHAPTER 2

If surfing brought this on me, I couldn't be the only one that felt this way. However, in this day and age, when everybody's so busy with work and trying to build a family, where was I supposed to find people that were just as dedicated to understanding this feeling as me. At my local line up in Huntington Beach, it's very close to a city, and most people are just weekend warriors. Surfing is definitely a passion in a lot of people's lives, and there were some that are dedicated to the pursuit of its core, but a lot of them were just kids that had too much time on their hands.

Where were the core people that were tapping into the source? I have grown up reading surf magazines and seeing pictures of far off destinations. Beautiful tropical locations full of indigenous people riding broken boards, most likely left by professional surfers. If the Wiseman and Messiahs were homeless, in line cloths, and meditating on hills in far off destinations...... then I must seek them out. So first I traveled to Mexico.

Most of the time when traveling, I get distracted by the usual things. First I got to find a good wave, then I got to find a good drink, then I got to find a pretty local girl and try my luck. I spent some time surfing in Cabo San Lucas at a place called shipwrecks, only to get wrapped up in a party and go home with a mean hangover. I met a lot of Texas folk, local Mexican surfers, and pretty girls from all over the world. But for the most part I was in a black out half the time having the time of my life and forgetting about my mission.

When I got home I was so broke, that I had to go back to work and recover financially. I also had to start a new plan because I had forgotten the original mission. It was time to start planning the next adventure.

For every surfer when the waves get cold in California, if you want to get something tropical, big, and worth it, you go to Hawaii. Hawaiians are the original Kings of surfing. They are our own royalty and should have a lot of respect paid to them...especially when you are in the land of aloha.

For most people, when they go to Hawaii they book a hotel and sip a couple mai tais on the beach before checking out a couple of spots like pearl harbor, crossing the North Shore from the safety of the sand. For me, I didn't have the luxury of money to drop on a $200 a night hotel. I didn't even pack a board because the waves in Hawaii require such a distinctive different type of board that I figured I would just get one when I get there.

I had stayed in Kauai with a friend's uncle a couple years previous where I had the key to the city and a car. For this trip, I just kind of landed in Hawaii on the island of Oahu with a backpack. I crashed with a friend that I had met years before, but his girlfriend was kind of an uptight human, especially with me being there, so I ended up going downtown and purchasing a tent and hopped the bus to the North Shore.

I stayed the first night in a hostel called three tables. I started to meet some super cute girls that were extraordinarily distracting and I did not want to make the same mistake as I did in Mexico, so I ended up leaving the hostel after the first night. I found a local park and slept in it the first night before exploring an entire day in the area for a spot to pitch my tent in the jungle.

I can't give away the location in which I found, because I don't want to blow up the spot. But I ended up thinking I was being clever by saving a bunch of money and sleeping in a tent, in a place that I thought nobody knew about. The first night I was drinking a bunch of beer by myself and passed out in the tent. I woke up in the morning to all of my beer missing. As I checked around I didn't see any tracks or any trace of people. It had mysteriously disappeared in the middle of the night.

"Menehunes brah!" Said the surf shop worker; who must have been about 55 years old when I was renting a board by Shark Cove. "The what?" I asked after explaining to him that my beer went missing. "Menehunes are a type of Hawaiian leprechaun figure in local folklore. Those little bastards steal everything!" To be completely honest the last thing I thought when my beer went missing, was that a mythical creature had taken it. As I was believing that this man had maybe a little bit too much sun while he was surfing one day and started seeing midgets that are thieves around the island, he threw me a water bottle that had a picture of a little Hawaiian guy on it and it was a local company called Menehunes!

After talking to a couple of people in the water while at Rocky point, gas chambers, and a couple of other breaks that I did not know the name of, I found that almost everybody on the island believed in these little shits. I thought nothing of it and proceeded to go get myself another 18 pack before journeying back into the jungle to where my tent was set up.

When I got back to my tent there was a six pack waiting in front of it. I had nothing but questions at this point. Were these mythological creatures thieves? Or just borrowers? I mean they did drink my beer in the middle of the night, but they had somehow purchased more and left it by my tent in the afternoon. I thought nothing of it and began to consume most of the six pack before passing out around 4 o'clock in the afternoon.

I woke up a little bit groggy because I was tired from surfing and probably did not hydrate before completely re-toxing my system with the newly found beer by my tent. As I was pulling myself together I could smell a smell in the air that was all too familiar. In Hawaii they call it "Pakalolo"

" Thanks for the brews mate!" I heard from outside of my tent as two people walked by blowing smoke in the air. I peeked my head out to see two very tan human beings that must've been about 22 to 23, with overgrown beards especially for their age.

"Was that you guys? Thanks for buying more for me. All the locals told me that I got jacked by a couple leprechauns!" The two of them laughed at me "You mean menehunes? Those little bastards will jack you but they're not gonna return the favor like we did mate!"

The two gentlemen had very thick Australian accents, and I invited them to my camp to hang out as they shared their smoke with me. As it turns out, the two of them have been living in a similar area not far from my tent for almost 2 years. That's one of the reasons I did not want to blow up the spot, there was actually a large community of tents spread out throughout the entire area. Here I thought I was being smart and clever, not having to pay for a hotel. This was a very unoriginal idea in the surfing world. Luckily Hawaii doesn't care as much as long as you don't litter or trash the area and you respect the locals.

I ended up surfing with these guys for a couple of days and realizing that they were complete nut jobs. They paddled me out and some surf that was well beyond anything I thought I would ever paddle out in. But after getting to know them for the couple of weeks I was there, these guys were on the same mission I was. They did not care about society, politics, TV shows, or sports. What these guys were all about, was the feeling they kept chasing when riding waves and living in nature. "The stoke" they called it. I've heard that in Hollywood movies, surf videos, and even interviews with pros. But I never heard people describe it as a lifestyle.

These guys did not care about retirement, or some type of bank account. They ate fruit off the trees, fished for their food and the only thing they had to spend their money on was water because there wasn't really a super clean local source in the area except for when it rained. When it did rain, they had rain collectors. And once again after a couple weeks I started to get to know a couple other people in the area, these were not people that were like me, vacationing for a couple of weeks. They have been there for years. Surfing their guts out during the winter, and making money during the summer in Honolulu.

There was one guy that I met there who had been living this way for around 15 years. He had a nice little set up in a tree, and all he cared about was riding waves. Is this what I was to become? Was I headed in this direction? Was I about to be a "surf bum?" Here I thought I was tapping into something spiritually unique, and what I was discovering is that people literally give up everything in their entire life to chase this feeling. I was looking into the future of this and it seemed a little bit scary.

It's not that I wanted my life to look like a music video, I'm a much simpler person than that. But I'm not sure if wiping my ass with banana leaves for the rest of my life was on the agenda either. So in a way, "The stoke" was just as addicting as drugs? I have grown up in a family full of drug attic's and they chased that high their entire life only to end up poor and dried out. These people have peace in their eyes that I've only seen and born again Christians and Hare Krishna people. Drug attic's looked more like lost people, the people in Hawaii looked more "found" then lost when I looked in their eyes.

It was a confusing conundrum and I could not figure out what I was heading towards. Was I to be a bum who lived in the bushes and rode the bliss of a stoke feeling? Was I to look like a bum the rest of my life who had a secret that the rest of society could not understand? This again left me with more questions than answers.

The flight home had me feeling extremely confused, and when I landed at LAX, I was belligerently drunk while racking my mind trying to figure out what the hell it was that I was doing. The next day of course, the first thing I did was wake up and go surfing. No matter how confusing it was, the first thing I did was go chase that stoke.

At this point I started to understand that nothing else began to matter.

I couldn't be the only one that felt like this once again. As someone who didn't want to be a bum, but also did not wanna go into slavery of society and lose the stoke, was there a balance to this religion.... to the society sabotage of success in my peers eyes.... to what most people would consider madness? It could not be all or nothing could it? Could the "stoke" be a way to describe some type of religious enlightenment?

I had to figure out how far back in history this goes, so I started heading to the drawing board and the search.

CHAPTER 3

In a world of time and money, living in the moment is something of a luxury usually reserved for the very rich and the dirt poor. The majority of people today will wake up when the alarm clock goes off at 6am and hit the snooze button before getting ready for the traffic jam. I drive by the 405 freeway at 9am and see a line of cars in every lane as far as I can see in each direction.

Most of the cars I see are full of people who went to grade school for 13 years, college for 4 years, and have now landed a job. I see people sit in a cubicle for 9 hours a day only to return home in the traffic that started their day in the opposite direction. The itinerary for the mass majority of people once they get home, is to stop at a fast food drive thru to grab a meal before arriving at home to eat while watching their favorite shows on T.V.. It's not that my routine is any different at times. I myself have done what I call falling asleep to reality, or selling my soul for money. It seems to me like a trap that society has placed on itself in order to keep progression flowing like some kind of machine where people volunteer themselves as the fuel.

Society itself these days, with the connection people have through phones and the Internet, can appear to be like a living organism. And if you're not part of the machine, then you're lost in its tracks. I myself have tried to blend in with the social expectations of society. But there's just one problem....I'm a surfer.

As a surfer, my clock doesn't revolve around the regular 9 to 5 schedule of your average weekend warrior. Instead, my clock revolves around seasons, high and low tides and pressures on a barometric scale. I live by wind speeds and far off storms thousands of miles away.

When I read about great prophets and Messiahs, it is my understanding that most of them were of humble means. When one pictures a wise man, it's not a king, or a businessman. When depicted, the wisest of men is wrapped in very little cloth meditating on a mountain top far from civilization.

The followers of saviors and prophets do their best to follow the teachings of peace and prosperity left for the generations to obtain nirvana, enlightenment, or the key to heaven. The guidelines mentioned by the most famous and revered were from Jesus Christ, Krishna, Mithera, and the Buddha. Most of these guidelines are all as similar in nature as they are in common sense:

Do not kill

Do not steal

Do not envy

Do not covet

Do not sell your soul

Help all In need

Share, do not be greedy

Do not lay with another's spouse

Do not fall into temptation

And so on.....

Most of the rules are simply taught or learned by the age of 5. And most are not followed by the age of 25, even though this is the age when they apply the most. I see the modern world of business based entirely on greed.

In business, the object is to obtain the most profitable endeavors possible. Sharing those profits would be a sin in the business community. Sure you hear about philanthropy done in the name of charity. But if you take a closer look you'll see most of it is a business proposition for taxes.

A man can spend his entire life climbing the corporate ladder. Spending years in school obtaining a certificate, only to spend the rest of his life groveling at the feet of the corporate hierarchy. All while working in a cubicle everyday so that he can afford his 30 year fixed rate loan on his house mortgage.

The word "mortgage" itself is derived from a "Law French " term used in the middle ages by lawyers meaning "Death Pledge". These days, a mortgage can mean to tie yourself to a bank for up to 30 years or face losing the security of your home.

By spending your entire life in a cubicle or under the thumbnail of a corporate machine, you are essentially selling your soul for the temptation of money. Sure, you get two weeks a year that you get to fly to Hawaii and pretend you are free. But at the end of the day, you still have to get back to that bank loan debt. Back to your life of slavery where it takes coffee to keep the mice running on the wheels in place, and alcohol to numb the pain of a stagnant life.

Society does run off of this idea that we are free to do as we please. But in this day and age money is king. It's been told for thousands of years "He who has the gold, makes the rules." The idea that money is real has blinded man since its comprehensive discovery.

Perhaps the idea of detachment from such a worldly thing as money sounds crazy to the corporate ladder climber. This may be because while sitting in traffic on the way to work, he saw a man sitting on the on ramp of the freeway. And as he read the sign asking for anything he could spare, he rolled up his window and hid his wallet while thinking "Get a job you bum. I have one, this is my pile and I earned it. I'll never be like you."

"You see there are three classes of people in America. There's the upper class, that do none of the work, pay some of the taxes, and keep most of the money. There's the middle class, that do all of the work, pay most of the taxes, and keep some of the money. Then there's the lower class like the homeless that are there, just to scare the hell out of the middle class. You know, to keep them showing up to those jobs on Monday." -George Carlin

There have been social experiments to see the reaction difference between the have and the have nots, and the results have been quite surprising. The experiment, where a man with a cane posed as a blind man. He would walk past people dropping a $50 bill to see the truth of greed. The man would walk by people in business suits, and then walk by homeless people.

As the "blind man" walked by people in business attire and dropped the money, 9 times out of 10, the man in the suit would pick up the money, put it in his pocket and walk away. The times he walked by homeless people, 9 times out of 10 the homeless people would stop and return the money to the "blind man".

Perhaps, the people selling their soul for the time spent at work while chasing the temptation of money, can be hypnotized so by it's effect, that greed becomes part of the process. Or perhaps the people who had come before in ancient times to give the message of peace and lay the ground rules, saw into the heart of man. Even in ancient times an observant person could see that the pit of greed only grows with possession. The more they have, the more they want from a tree of money that bears no fruit.

" The key to happiness, is the reduction of desires."- Krishna

"It is easier for a camel to fit through the eye of a needle, than it is for a rich man to enter heaven." -Jesus Christ

When asked " What thing surprises you most about humanity?" The Dali Lama then responded " Man, because he sacrifices his health in order to make money. Then, he sacrifices money to recuperate his health. And then he is so anxious about the future that he does not enjoy the present; the result being that he does not live in the present or the future; he lives as if he is never going to die, and then dies having never really lived. "

Life is a massive mystery, and to not recognize this, would be a sin against yourself. A man who chases money his whole life, seems to live as if he'll never die. It's almost like his objective is to die with the biggest pile of material and that will make him happy. But what of happiness is a destination? It's purely a State of mind.

According to modern studies, not all, but most people who are rich suffer from some type of depression. Wealth can seem to fill a void but only for a brief time. Now I can admit that being depressed in a Lamborghini might feel a bit better than being depressed at a bus stop, but the fact that we feel depressed in the first place is where my thought process begins.

" Certain things will capture your eye, but pursue only which captures your heart." - Native American proverb.

In the 21st century, it's close to impossible to try to live without some type of pursuit of money. It is after all a "Necessary evil", but wouldn't that only be true in a world where evil is necessary? After all, if the Wiseman is happiest atop a mountain in a state of zen meditation, then how is tieing your soul into a system of self-slavery in the pursuit of happiness the answer? From this perspective, if working a 40 hour week in an office for money is what makes you happy, then a happy journey to you. For the rest of us, especially surfers, we've redefined our definition of happiness.

Just as a Wiseman sitting in stillness under a tree can find "nirvana", so too can an everyday surfer find a zen state of mind in even the smallest of waves. It's been labeled "Surf bum" in the past by society. These are people who sell everything they own to devote a life to the ocean.

Greg Noll was a surfer in the 1950's and 60's. He talks about a life at the beach, where all he did was surf his guts out. He's best known for his incredible surf on the wave of the century at Makaha. But the lifestyle he and his companions lived was, at the time, anything but normal.

In the 1950's through the early 1980's there was a lifestyle in surfing culture that was widely misunderstood. While the rest of the people were busy building the country, there was a tribe of people camped out on the beach soaking up the rays of life. These "surf bums" were masked by the media as social outcasts that were nothing more than drunken beach bums causing mayhem. Greg Noll reflects on the times "We'd spend all day at the beach just surfing, it's all we did. We were like screw the money, we're having as much fun as we could possibly have....what else did we need?"

In these times it was easy to set up camp on the beach and no one would bother you. It was a serious state of zen that wasn't touched by the world of money yet. It was just something you did and enjoyed purely. There was no scoreboard, no audience on the beach, it was just you and the ocean. It may not be a man in a loincloth atop a mountain meditating but to me it's pretty close.

"In search of the Buddha, if you find him in the road, kill him" - zen master

The life of a modern day surfer is a lot more acceptable to society now that we have an official industry. We have an entire culture based on money from the millions brought in by the clothing and board industry, not to mention some of the highest paid athletes in the world. The image of a surfer has certainly changed in the last fifty years but the feeling still remains.

Every surfer in a Sunday morning Huntington beach crowded line up, is still in pursuit of the zen like feeling obtained in a good session on their favorite board. They are out there in January when the water is hyperthermic, and when there's no sign of swell. They're out there even if there's a shark sighting in the nearby area. None of these surfers are getting paid for this, nor will it help with life expenses, taxes or family problems. It's done for love of the ocean, it's done for state of mind. Like an artist who paints a picture for free as his canvas disintegrates, it's done for the feeling and nothing else. It's purity at its finest, it's purely Zen.

CHAPTER 4

In Most times, before the last hundred years or so, there was a connection humans had to their activities not seen today. For all the rest of human history, things we take for granted in modern times, were the missing link to that connection. Something like eating on a daily basis was a ritual of survival.

In the past, if you wanted to eat, you had to go hunting, whether for berries to pick or animals to kill, you were always on the prowl for your next meal. Something that the modern day person at a McDonalds Drive thru would know nothing about. If you needed meat, you grabbed your spear, and went in search of animals to kill, so you could live. Half of the time, hunting was liable to get you killed.

In Africa, there is a tribe of people who still practice a form of hunting known as "Kudu"in which the hunter chases the prey on foot until the animal can run no more, and collapses in exhaustion. The human body can out run all other life on earth because we are equipped with the longest running endurance. Humans can run from sun up to sun down if need be. The tribes that practice this form of hunting describe it as one of the most rewarding and sacred. Besides the runners high that we are all familiar with, they say that the mental reward for your kill is the most worth it once achieved. It is at times considered a test from the deities and the pride and peace felt was a holy gift.

The plains people native to North America, hunted buffalo for thousands of years on foot before the introduction of horses by the Europeans. For them, the thrill of the hunt was just as sacred. There were ceremonies, rituals, and dances, all just for the preparation of such hunts. These natives also prided themselves in the fact that when done successfully, it was the most rewarding experience known besides having children. And both were considered a gift from the heavens.

Both of these tribes that are known for their archaic style of hunting, seem to say that the reward is worth the risk. I'm not suggesting that we all start sharpening sticks, and chasing squirrels in our local parks. What I am saying is that for thousands of years, we had a direct connection with our food and a reward system in our brain that made us feel good about a successful meal.

The brain circuits are an important reward system for things such as food, music, exercise, and sex. All rewards of pleasure are met with a dose of dopamine in the brain. This is the reward system. It makes you feel good when you complete a task such as a hunt, or kiss the one you love, or even just eat a candy bar. Endorphins are the high you feel after intense exercises.

Other reward chemicals in the brain are serotonin, and oxytocin. Both are mostly the reward chemicals for the feeling of happiness, love, and social bonding, and all three are extremely addictive. In the defense of the ancient people who had no science for the explanation of these feelings, when experienced, they do feel quite heavenly.

Not only heavenly but highly addictive. Love for instance, is one of the most addicting chemicals the human brain can endure. When love is taken away in something like a divorce or a break up, people are so addicted to the feeling of love that they have withdrawls. The withdrawals are so intense that some people have even committed suicide during such episodes.

Another traditional chemical experience lies with just the anticipation of the hunt itself. There were a handful of mystical taboos and superstitions that were prominent during the waiting period of "just before the hunt." This too was a healthy dose of dopamine. Anticipation of the reward was sometimes a larger buildup in the reward itself.

In these hunting scenarios the hunter would run down the prey and get a dose of dopamine as he catches it. He would then proudly bring it back to his tribe that oxytocin and serotonin made him feel connected to. He would then feast with them for another dose of dopamine from food and all while the endorphins were rushing through his veins from the exertion of the hunt. Not to mention the addiction of the adrenaline from facing whatever beast he killed. It's been joked by Joe Rogan, a comedian, that oxytocin is the chemical that stops humans from eating their babies when the food runs short. (Not relevant but I found it funny)

Since our reward system has been set on overdrive throughout all of human history for such things as simply obtaining a meal on a daily basis, it's no wonder that these days, so much depression plaques our modern day society. Without the rewards from the brain, there's no true feelings of happiness. As thrilling as the drive thru at your favorite fast food restaurant may be, you're not going to feel the satisfaction of the hunt. There's just no thrill, and no connection that can match our primal desire for the right chemical balance of satisfaction.

People still try to find ways to create small glimpses of our most basic mental and chemical rewards. Some will watch a scary movie, or people will jump from an airplane, just to have it. There are a galaxy of recreational thrill seeking experiences that have been invented to recreate the feeling that our body has a symbiotic relationship with. In my opinion the best known for me is the sport, or lifestyle, or even religion of surfing.

Religion is defined as " A pursuit or interest in which someone ascribes supreme importance in a particular system of faith and/or worship." This may not mean much to people who don't surf when they look at the image that Hollywood has created for surfers. With such an example of Spicoli in "Fast times at Ridgemont high" most people think of stoners in VW BUSES with skateboards and long hair. Not saying that this wasn't a real image especially in the 1970-80s. But surfing's roots go deeper than then the ghetto Dogtown boys.

Ancient Polynesians lived a lifestyle so simple that many styles of recreation were created to pass the time in between fishing and making POI. There was no more sacred religious activity than what they called "HE'E NALU" , which is Hawaiian for surfing. To them, the ocean was the holiest of places. The religion of these ancient people was almost entirely based on water from the ocean and fire from the active volcanoes that created the islands they inhabited.

To these people, surfing was so sacred that it even had a hierarchy. For example, if a peasant were to drop in on the same wave as someone who was of royal blood, then that person was allowed to kill the peasant the moment they reached the beach. The act of riding waves was so sacred to these people, that the insult of interrupting even one wave was at times serious and fatal.

What is it about the lifestyle of surfing that has such a grip on those who pursue a lifelong journey of oceanic expression? Why is it that just as sacred as the ancient Polynesians held it in their religious beliefs, that modern day surfers can hold it dear to their hearts? What is different about surfers that are misunderstood by Hollywood and people who have never tapped into the culture so much that it leads to the saying that "On a surfer knows the feeling"?

It has been argued for centuries about what religious beliefs are correct, so much so that wars have been waged based upon different ideas for how we were created, where we come from, where humanity is going, and how it will end. The anxiety of these questions have caused families to break up, countries to build walls, and death on an incalculable scale throughout history.

People seem to worry so much about where they come from, where they're going, and who's right or wrong about this that they very seldom enjoy the present moment. Philosophy says that the heaven that most are searching for, I is in the moment. That happiness is a lifestyle instead of a destination.

Monks say that they find heaven or a state of nirvana through meditation and yoga in the stillness. While the tribes of Africa and North America say they found it in the sacred hunting rituals, and religious people say they find it in prayer. These are all forms of living in the present. A prayer or meditation is a way to focus inwardly while not worrying about the minutiae of daily life even if just for the time spent in silence. The hunting rituals of the native people was a focus on the direct moment laid out in front of the situation at hand. The chemical mixed in the brain, along with the will to eat and live, was the addiction to these moments.

When a surfer begins his journey to become a waterman, it is a long and dangerous endeavor. He begins by stepping out of his element and into the water. At times, depending on the location, he joins the ocean and shares it with fish the size of a limousine that is equipped with razor sharp teeth made for tearing through flesh. Now, not all surfers need to worry about sharks due to the fact that there are millions of surfers and about 5 deaths a year due to attacks, but it's always in the back of the mind of everyone in the water who has seen the movie "JAWS".

The average surfer takes about 4 years to learn to truly surf. It can be a long and death defying journey just to achieve surfer status. The reason it is so long of a journey is because with every other sport or lifestyle, you begin standing up or already going. In surfing, before you can ride a wave you must first learn to relax in an element that is constantly changing. They must learn to properly paddle, duckdive, relax when you take sets on the head, figure out your stance (goofy or natural), understand the currents and tides, relax on a wipeout, which waves are rideable, where to be on the wave, where the wave is catchable, how far out to sit, how to drop in, where your feet should be on the board, what kind of board is right for you, what kind of board is right for the conditions, how to relax while being chased down by a wall of water, how to relax when the elements are out of your limitations, and did I mention that you need to learn to relax? Once you stand up and understand these things, surfing is the easy part.

Learning to start surfing can be hard work but it's also extremely rewarding. Just as the hunters in Africa and North America, your exertion will be met with a flood of endorphins from the exercise. And furthermore, when you have to learn a lot of new things in order to catch waves, it will certainly be met with high doses of dopamine when achieved.

Dopamine, adrenaline, oxytocin, and serotonin are all chemicals that mix to make you feel good. When you feel good it is easier to live in the moment. When surfing, you are causing these chemicals to mix and this causes you to enjoy or "live in the moment."

As you sit in the lineup on any day, you are tapping into a feeling that has been wired into your psyche and reward system for thousands of years of evolution. You are a hunter of waves. When the waves come, you have to sit dangerously in the impact zone just to chase the wave down. You have to fight the urge your body is giving out that says that you are going to drown. You have to chase the waves like a hunter chasing prey. As you catch and make the wave, the reward system goes off in your mind, feeding it the same "feel good" chemicals as a hunter who makes the kill. You then become the hunter that your brain is hardwired to be. When the ride is done, you are now equipped with the necessary chemicals that feed your primordial instinct to feel alive.

In the surf community, it can certainly feel like a tribal atmosphere. We have our legends and mystical traditions. Along with our own tall tales of the places we've been and waves we caught. When I meet a real surfer, they are instantly my brother or sister. This common bond & at times makes me feel like I'm meeting a family member for the first time. It's a religious fellowship of people dedicated to chasing the thrill of the hunt. The hunt for waves.
All the chemicals that are in the brain make you feel good are highly addictive. Adrenaline junkies are called junkies for a reason. Love junkies are exactly the same. The people who risk it all for love, live for that butterfly feeling in the stomach and that heart pounding of that first kiss. And just like heartbreak, when the ocean is taken away from the waterman, he mourns her. It's hard to describe when you've never felt it…. You just have to feel it to understand. No words in poetry can describe it, just like falling in love. It's gotta be felt.

"The wave hunter sits in stillness (relaxed) on his surfboard. He feels the water surrounding his body, and the wind blowing on his face. The anticipation of the hunt for waves on his mind. The natural elements are unforgiving, the pain in his arms from the paddle out causing his heart to race, his eyes to focus, and his nerves to shake. As the beast approaches the hunt is on. He scratches the surface as the forces of energy begin a flight or fight instinct. He chooses to fight as the monster rears up and allows him to choose his fate.

 "Not this time!" Says the hunter as he casts himself over the ledge in a dance of do or die. The hunter then becomes the hunted as the force tries to swallow him whole. In the belly of the beast the hunter must decide, be swallowed and chewed up by the coral teeth, or hold on for dear life and fight his way toward the light at the end of the tunnel."

CHAPTER 5

So if it was the reward systems I was after, I was closer to a drug addict then I thought. In old fashioned opium dens of Chinese culture, you would smoke the tar-of the plant that was highly addictive. The first high was always considered the best one you will ever have. After that, you chase a feeling of that first time for the rest of your addiction. The Chinese used to call it "Chasing the Dragon" and a lot of people died in its pursuit.

Drug attics chase the dragon on a regular basis, they get so high that nothing else matters. This in itself is a trick on your reward system. The very same reward system that kept us alive since the dawn of life. It's meant to have us chase food and sex in order to keep Life moving in a cycle of eating and reproducing. Just like the Hawaiians, we have become so successful that we have begun to create our own problems and play with our own reward systems for recreation.

So by this narrative the feeling I was getting from surfing, was just my primordial reward system making me feel complete? Was it just that simple in scientific terms? Or was there something more to it all? Maybe something spiritual?

I can tell you what was not spiritual. The fact that when I got home from Hawaii I went back to work as a truck driver. The looped schedule rotated Monday through Friday and made a year ago by extremely fast because of its routine. Surfing was always there for me in the morning and I was gaining skill very rapidly because of the consistency in which I was practicing my craft.

But once again as humans become satisfied, I became hungry. I want longer waves, I wanted deeper barrels, I wanted more of a challenge. Perhaps I just wanted to get higher. Perhaps once you reach a certain point you have to keep pushing further in order to fill that physical need of your reward systems. Or perhaps my spirit was trying to set itself free and wanted to fly. Whether it was physical or spiritual, the hunger became real.... to chase this Dragon ....a little bit further.

At work, my job began to feel Mandane. The people I worked with began to seem like robots. They were happy with their little pile of dopamine they were getting on Fridays. My conversations were shorter with people and my mind was wandering further. This pursuit was definitely requiring something more so I began to surf contests.

I've always enjoyed watching the contests on line where Kelly Slater dominated for about the last 25 years. You can see the progression and the latest tricks that the most skilled surfers were doing. The aerial maneuvers were getting ridiculous in nature and complexity. Where people were once satisfied with a guy doing rail to rail surfing, guys were doing Supermans, Ariel 360s and even 540s to keep people entertained. It was becoming extremely exciting with the onset of the dream tour instead of the world tour.

Now it was the longest way imaginable, the heaviest wave you've ever seen, the most perfect surf on the planet. Every stop was some type of new scale That had to be topped every year. People were bored with sand bottom brakes and three turns, they wanted 10 turns and guys going face first into shallow reefs from 20 foot faces. I had begun to notice that I was not the only one chasing the Dragon. The progression of the sport of surfing was full of it in every direction.

I had practiced contests and watched diligently at what the score systems were all about. I had to adjust my surfing from something of joy to something of what I knew the judges were looking for. After a couple of years, I had begun to do well at local amateur contests. I had mastered a 360 and that seemed to score and get me through heats on a regular basis.

In 2015 I won my first contest, it was nothing of world tour level but to me it was a bucket list accomplishment that had me chasing more. I've been pursuing it further and ended up winning the entire series. Once again nothing big that won a bunch of money, but it was enough for me to get a thrill. I was chasing another Dragon and I was perfecting my craft in a different way. It was keeping me going and what made me open my eyes in the morning. I hit the ground running every day in pursuit of points on a scoreboard that a judge gave me based on the fact that I had figured out what it was he was looking for.

After winning an entire series in Huntington Beach of an amateur surfing contest for the summer, I was so high that regular surfing for joy just didn't do it for me. I had to perfect my moves, I had to be better, quicker, faster, harder. By the next year I was so worked up that winning was all I cared about. It's what gave me my dopamine. So with the high came the crash.

In 2016, I had almost no interest in surfing a contest unless I was winning. At the time I started to feel some type of shift in my consciousness. Once winning became the only thing I focused on, I started to become depressed. I stopped surfing contests and even surfing for recreation. I would go to the beach and sit on a bench, and just stare at the ocean. Like a drug attic that could not get his fix. Something had to change, I wasn't stoked anymore.

What is a dragon slayer to do when there's no more dragons left to slay? He goes on a quest. An adventure. For me I ended up out in the middle of the desert at some type of psychedelic electronic music festival where I ate a bunch of LSD and it told me to give up everything and to go on a journey. I couldn't do it right away but I had a direction to chase a different type of high ....just the thought of it, got me going.

In the following months, work had become like a prison to me. Conversations have become nails on a chalkboard with anybody that wasn't talking about spiritual pursuit, or some type of stuff they were chasing, and talking about it with passion. In short, I need to do something radical and Transformative.

One day I was working, and it all hit me at once like a nervous break-down. I broke down in my truck and began to ball my eyes out, out of nowhere. It wasn't even a particularly bad day, my soul had just had enough and reached its limit. And I wanted to break free so I quit my job as soon as I got back to the office.

Was this a spiritual experience? I thought spiritual experiences were supposed to be good? Maybe this is good? The thoughts that run through my head we're not only of surfing, but of Adventure as well. All of the great stages and Wiseman had some type of journey that they did along the way. Something tells me that their life wasn't all peaches and cream for them to decide to give up everything and just go.

On paper everything looked perfect, I had my place by the beach, I had a job that paid well, I was doing good and contests, I had a good love life.... but something was missing. Some type of connection, it seemed, was reaching out to me. Was this God? Was surfing becoming my new religion? I have no answer to any of my questions. It was almost like the people that have gone through this, were already out there and I had to go meet them. I had to figure out if it was the stoke, or if we were all just crazy and we were going to end up homeless bums oneday asking for change.

But where was I supposed to go? Do I just drop everything and start walking? Every place had already been discovered. So there wasn't a boat to just jump on as a volunteer explorer, nor could I hop on horseback and just start riding west with the wagon Trail. I was exploring my reward systems through surfing, my consciousness through psychedelics, And I was beginning to understand the hitchhikers that I used to pick up that were hippies, and I was beginning to understand them well. I had to go somewhere but I didn't know where. All I knew was I was done with this job and I had to go. But where?

CHAPTER 6

I am convinced that the expansion and eventual globalization of the human species is due to the fact that man has been trying to be free since the very first hierarchy. It seems like the establishment of government, taxes, and laws that make no sense, and are only in place for political reasons, are a disease to the human freedom mindset. I believe that surfing is the first world's last Frontier of freedom within the human psyche.

Of course the expansion of the human species is much more complicated than just looking for freedom in the early days of tribal living. Some were searching for the best hunting grounds, some were curious explorers, and some were just caught in a wanderlust hoping for greener pastures. But as wanders gathered into tribes, and tribes joined up for both survival and procreation reasons, they eventually became villages, or small cities.

In a place like a city or a village where large numbers of people gather together, there has to be order. Order is a good thing for the safety and wellbeing of the people. Without it, there would surely be chaos. But there's a funny thing that happens when you give people authority over one another. Authority is usually created to protect people from themselves or each other. However, with authority comes power, and power for some reason or another always is abused and often turns corrupt.

Most laws set by man are in the name of keeping the herd safe. But once a system is set in place and authority is given power, it will without a doubt be abused. Such as the saying goes by John Emerich Edward Dalberg Acton "Absolute power corrupts absolutely."

By giving people power over other people and creating a hierarchy, this gives way to positions of power to be abused. The more laws set in place, the more power is created for the system that becomes the ruling party in a heavily populated village or city. Usually, this gives way to another system that is in charge of keeping the current system in line. But giving more power to control power essentially it's like a snake eating its own tail.

I feel like as these systems become corrupt, the people who see the original vision and are unhappy with the circumstances, begin to flee the controlled area. Systems in which corruption leads to such things as taxation, imprisonment, and a ruling party bent on making "their" special interest the norm.

But as these people leave the cities of corruption and venture out to seek new beginnings, they become no more than seeds of the system. This is true because once on their own, they must find other nomads to trade with, learn from, and to mate. They must also join alliances to survive in the wild, giving way to the start of a new small village that gives way to a larger village that will eventually become a city. A city of corruption and greed in which some people will grow tired of and leave the cities to seek out a new beginning and the cycle starts over.

Over time, the land runs out and gives way to coastlines where there is no more land to run from the impending corruption. And the ever-expanding villages turn to cities, and the cities become empires that establish armies and create Wars in the name of God and country. And with Empires and armies come more laws, more taxes, and less freedom. The nomads run completely out of land and become outcasts for not conforming to the laws of the societies created by the corrupt hierarchies.

The outcasts, usually in the form of Nomads or indigenous people, unwilling to conform to a lawful Society, eventually are seen as a threat to these systems. This happens because people who see the system as an infection in the human psyche or brainwash, say that you need people to constantly watch your safety for a price known as a tax, refuse to pay that tax and live a life on their own terms. This freedom mindset is not beneficial to the eventual totalitarian system that is an Empire. A system that requires only tax paying obedient workers and soldiers.

Over thousands of years you see empires rise up, conquer, and fall. The fall is usually due to the fact that the bigger the empire, the more corrupt the system. It's a history that repeats again and again, never learning from the previous mistakes of the past. Even the discovery of America is a perfect time lined example of how it works.

After the Conquistadors of Spain ravage through the Americas looking for gold and creating genocide along their way, the indigenous nomadic like people who occupied the lands begun to see the system and its power destroy their free way of life. Settlers began to travel to America to get away from the corruption of Europe and its churches. People like the Protestants who protested the Catholic Church arrived in America to worship as they saw fit.

But as settlers began to establish villages in The Villages began to grow into cities, the systems they ran from, began to bloom within the systems they created. As this began to happen, people began to see that as cities turned to colonies, the laws and taxes that they were running from were as present as the lands they were trying to avoid.

When people saw this system installing itself into every area of the land that the colonies established, they began running west from it. People ran West from the system as it followed them to the coast. Once settlements reached the coast, the system was not far behind and at this time it was building a railroad to travel faster to establish its rule. Once established, the system began by creating laws and slaughtering the indigenous people or anybody that would not conform or be a contributor to society.

But nowadays with the four corners of the earth completely discovered, conquered, and systems put in place that are set for corruption in a globalization of money power and greed, there is nowhere else to run from it. The people that do are called hobos, tramps, or bums. The American Eagle that was supposed to represent freedom has now dug its deadly talons into the lives of the 9 to 5 slaves and obedient tax-paying workers.

One indigenous people that was taken over by the system of the United States, was in a chain of islands in the Pacific Ocean called Hawaii. When Captain James Cook discovered these islands he wrote many times in his journals and logs about their freedom of way of life. They had such freedom because the food was abundant. This left time in their day-to-day lives for things like Recreation. One of these recreational activities, was known as "He'enalu" or surfing.

As James Cook wrote in his logs, surfing was an activity of the utmost Joy and freedom. Most Hawaiians, men and women would surf in the nude. It was an artistic expression of oneself that was surrounded by Hawaiian religion and respectful love for the ocean.

But as history goes, the sport of surfing was put to rest by the Christian Church, due to the easy mixing of nude sexes, and its apparent lack of contribution to society. There was no fun allowed in a world now discovered by a church that was saving Souls in a system bent on creating profit.

It took almost a hundred years before surfing came back on the scene. The only reason it did was because of a man named Alexander Hume Ford, who saw its potential for making money as a tourist attraction to Hawaii. As the system destroyed surfing for religious reasons, so too did it reinvented for-profit.

With the rediscovery of surfing, it was spread on a global scale by a Hawaiian Olympic swimmer by the name of Duke Kahanamoku. He spread the sport of Surfing by demonstrating it in places like California, New York, and Australia. The new recreational activity caught on quickly in places like California and Australia. In California, unlike it's Hawaiian tourist attraction roots, it became a lifestyle of rebellion in comparison to the capitalistic rat race that was America in the 1940s and 50s.

Kids labeled as hodads or surf bums, littered the beaches in self built shacks or just slept in the open on the sand. To a society that was putting itself into captivity by moving into suburban areas and only focusing on being "good little consumers", making a contribution to the very system that enslaves its participants in debt, this was a confusing choice to make. While the average person in America was focused on going to school, getting a career, buying a house and raising a family in a safe neighborhood, these beach bums seemed to find the satisfaction of contentment being poor and playing in the ocean all day. I believe that in a globalization of money, power, and greed, these so called bums found something that no 9 to 5 jobs, safety of housing in a neighborhood watch area, or large stacks of paper could buy. It was a discovery as old as time, since the first group of people gathered together and realized that with order comes corruption, and with power comes control. The very same people who left the villages and cities of ancient times to seek new beginnings would eventually be pushed to the edge of the map on the outskirts of society.

But somehow, where the land met the sea, they would again find the long sought after freedom they longed for, on 180 lbs Balsa wood boards. While being driven by waves on the ocean (The last Frontier) the last place where freedom can be found, it became frowned upon by those that are too afraid to taste it.

As surfing began to grow popular in the 1940s and 50s, even Hollywood could not ignore its charm. Such a mystery were these men and women who give up a regular life for one sleeping on the beach and living off pennies, that movie makers and writers had to take notice. This began what is known in the surfing world as "The post Gidget era."

Gidget was a Hollywood movie that tried to capture the essence of the "Surf bum way of life." The movie was about a young girl who gets tied up with surf bums and discovers their free way of life. It missed the soulful nature of the surfing spirit, but captured the popular imagination of the movie going audience.

The surfing world exploded after the "Post Gidget era" leading to over-crowded beaches and lineups. And with more people, as it does, came law and order. In Australia for certain beaches, if you wanted to ride a surfboard, you were required to purchase a permit to do so. Though it only lasted a few years, it was just another way to see how the system tried to take control of even the ocean once it ran out of land to control.

The way of life for surfers was eventually ended in such places as Australia and California by making laws for safety about sleeping on the beach. The advent of the lifeguard was the beginning of the end for surfing's nonconforming antisocial society. The further the surfers moved to find new spots, greener pastures, and the freedom to do as they pleased, the lifeguard state was not far behind to kick them off the now protected beach.

Eventually, even the coastlines ran out, leaving us surfers forced to move inland, get jobs and pay rent if we wanted to enjoy a taste of our way of life. It's ironic to me that the majority of people that live on the coastline don't even surf, especially considering the fact that it's the most expensive land in the developed world. It's almost as if the system knows that this is the Last Frontier of freedom and it wants us to pay to play.

All the land is now conquered, the coastlines are regulated, and we now essentially have to pay to play....and we do. The only true freedom these days that a surfer can enjoy while being tied down by an animalistic society of a system hell bent on destroying itself, is a 6am surf at your local break, just before work. It's the only place where we leave our cellphones in the car and we don't care what time it is. The only place where no matter the money in the bank, the bills that are due, or problems with people we may have, we can still escape. We can still, even if in tiny glimpses, feel the freedom that the human soul ultimately desires.

CHAPTER 7

Shane Dorian is a big wave surfer, and former world tour competitor who said it best in a few interviews I've read. "Surfing is a sport or a lifestyle that allows you to really stay young, even into your older age." It was this statement that I never understood until I began to grow into my older 20s.

Around the age of 25 I began to notice things about my friends that weren't surfers. I could see the loss of both innocence and shapely body. Of course, I had friends that would go to the gym, or do marathons, but the majority were having kids, diving into careers, and generally so to speak just becoming lazy in a life that requires sitting at a desk all day.

There's something different about wave hounds than your everyday average Joe. Most people will work all week and come Friday it's time to party. They sit around all Saturday running errands with a painful hangover and eventually just go home and nurse it until it's time for round 2. Sunday usually doesn't look any different. Surfers party as well. However, the next day we tend to burn it off in the water.

I think most surfers understand what I call "feeding the fish". It's that day after a rager, sitting in the water regurgitating the hangover bile and watching the guppies eat it. Somehow the waves always seem to get good when we're feeling our worst.

After years of this abuse, people who stay passionate about the lifestyle usually begin to go to sleep and wake up earlier to catch the morning glass. Of course, even this lifestyle isn't what makes you feel like a child inside. But it sure helps with the aging process of getting wasted every weekend.

As the saying goes "You're only as old as you feel." There's an array of activities and sales pitch ideas for staying younger looking like Botox, facelift, and copious amounts of off-the-shelf creams to put on your skin to unlock your "outer beauty". But what about your inner youth or child?

The most obvious and proven way to stay young is to stay in shape and disciplined with your eating habits & exercise. Other more mystical and still proven ways are yoga and meditation, finding your Chi or zen. Wiseman of eastern traditions talk about appreciating every second you're alive, and staying in the moment with everything you're capable of comprehending. Not easy to do in our world we are creating, where time is money and money is everything. It really doesn't leave room for appreciating the small stuff.

This is why we compare happiness in life to that of a child? Perhaps it's that they have no worries, so all they do is play all day. The innocence of a child is incomparable to any other type of happiness in the world. With no bills, no job, or deadlines all a child has to do is play. They make it up as they go along like an artist who paints a picture for themselves to enjoy, for no one else to view. There are no tests, no scores, or no judgment of any kind. Life is just one big playground for children.

The same is similar for surfers. Before I became a surfer, I would go as far as to say that my innocence was lost. I wanted to be either in the army, or be a missionary for the Christian

Church. When I was fifteen I moved to California, and the first thing I did was ask for a surfboard. My father bought me a $90 surfboard from a pawnshop.

I don't know what attracted me to the beach so much but it was powerful. I had no friends when I first moved out there, so everyday I would catch the 7am bus to the beach and surf all day and catch the 7pm bus home. The first year of surfing is always the hardest. The whole time you're learning everything every step of the way. You can generally tell how long a person has been surfing by how well they paddle. The embryonic stages of becoming a surfer is quite a tough one.

As you learn to paddle, duckdive, stay calm, ect, you will eventually catch your first wave. You can ask any surfer about their first wave and most of the time they tell you the story in vivid detail. I remember mine as clear as day. It was a gloomy July morning in seal beach. I'd be going to this beach everyday for a month and just getting tumbled in the shorebreak. The strangest part of the whole thing, was once it clicked, it seemed to flow together like I had known exactly what I was doing. As I reached my feet, time began to slow, and it was like I was viewing myself surfing from an angle I'd never experienced before. The level of ease that I put into it, was as if someone else who could surf well was controlling my body for me. After kicking out of my first wave, I was in disbelief at what had just occurred, as well as the emotions I was going through.

After catching that first wave, I then realized that I was the only person who was around. I was excited simply because of the fact that, not only was it hard work to get where I was, but it finally paid off in a way I never thought possible. There was no scoreboard or people on the beach watching...it was just me and the wave. And as time slowed down, in the pit of my stomach, I felt the most jovial feeling possible.

For that night and the next week I played the moment in my head over and over again, and every time I relived that moment it was with a childlike smile on my face and the utmost joy in my mind. The experience of my first wave was something I had to have again. I chased it, everyday until it happened again. Two weeks later, then one week later, then three days later, until it began to happen everytime I surfed.

Chasing this feeling that I was experiencing has become a staple in my life of my addiction. When I wake up in the morning it's mostly all I think about, just the thought of playing with the rolling balls of energy on the ocean that gives me a feeling that's unexplainable. To try and describe this feeling with human language would be an insult to its reality. The saying in the surfing world is that " Only a surfer knows the feeling" I found this term to be true because I can't put it into words, It could only be felt. Whatever it may be, I do say it makes you as happy as a child, and it's seeming to be highly addictive.

CHAPTER 8

There are times in life where the tide can get low, so to speak. By this, I mean the bills need payment, the relationships with people, whether love or friendship may be put on the rocks, and your job or career might suffer. These are the times when seeing that life is out of your control, and holding on through the storm is best understood. This is a time when you need to find your flow. If surfing is a religion, then flow is what you obtain as enlightenment.

They say the best way to flow is to let go. Of all the research and studying I've done in religious experience, flow states in action sports, and search for enlightenment, almost everything points to letting go. If you cling too tightly to anything, you become attached to that specific thing. When you're trying to float down the river with the flow of life, if you find attachment it's like hitting a rock or a tree. The flow is interrupted and chaos follows.

Every surfer knows the feeling of padding out in a beach break on a plus sized day. There are times when you time it just right. Then again, there are times when the struggle becomes real. The sinking feeling of making it to the impact zone just in time for the set of the day to roll in can be quite humbling. However, if you want to make it to the lineup, you have to weather the storm. Taking 6ft+ size waves on the head might be one of the most violent things one can experience. If the sets become increasingly consistent, every duck-dive, just keeping a grip on your board can feel like wrestling an alligator.

But the only constant in life is change. If you want to surf a bigger day, there's going to be a bigger reward, and even so a bigger consequence. But just like problems in life, you're going to have to learn to deal with these consequences, and understand that the set doesn't last forever.

If you take a wave on a bigger day, most likely you're going to be caught inside. This is the time to relax, know that you're not in control, only then can you ride out the storm. There are times that life can throw sets at you that seemed like at the time, will never end. But when you weather through the storm, and hold through the sets, that's the only way you'll be able to make it out and ride another wave.

In the summer of 2016, I had run into the crossroads of life. I had a job I hated, and a girl in my life that just wasn't for me. I'd begun to feel stuck. I was caught inside. So I quit my job, broke up with my girlfriend and flew to Costa Rica the next day.

I landed in San Jose, Costa Rica with just a backpack and no plan. No plan, so I could go with the flow. I found a website that had featured a hostel right on the beach by pavones, the wave I had flown down to surf. Turns out my geography was a bit off because Costa Rica has two similar hook shaped bays on the Pacific Coast and I simply chose the wrong one. Even so it was still on the beach. And there were waves.

I felt that being "caught inside" in life was wearing down on my soul. The reason for this trip was maybe to find an answer to it all. "Ask and you shall receive". I felt that if I went with the flow, no matter what happened, I would find my answers. I didn't have to search far. During the trip, the answer had found me.

I missed my flight that was to connect in Houston. This meant I had to wait from 7:30am to 9 o'clock pm at Lax for a flight to Florida that was two hours longer. I tried to be patient as much as one could while waiting for a 12hour layover for a longer connecting flight, but when you seek answers, and all roads seem to be blocked in every direction, it can leave you skeptical. All I could do was go with the flow.

After boarding my plane in Fort Lauderdale FL, I saw a person I had seen during my 5 hour layover in Florida. He boarded the plane and sat in front of me. He was an unmistakable looking figure. Covered in tattoos, a tall Native American look with bright blue eyes. He looked like a waterman, a large backpack with swim fins hanging off the side. I figured most people headed to Costa Rica were watermen, and as he sat in his seat, he gave me a nod as to say hello before we took off.

As I got off the flight and made my way through immigration, I had a guy from the hostel in Jaco picking me up. The line was almost two hours long and towards the end of it, as I looked back and saw the guy, there were a couple people behind me. Again a nod. I let a few people go ahead of me and had to begin a conversation with him at this point to see what he was about.

"How's it going?" I asked. As I threw out a shaka. "What's up man, how's it going?" He responded with the same. After talking for a few minutes, I found out that he was photographer Corey Patterson, here to shoot his business partner Tyler Crawford. I knew the name Tyler Crawford, I remember reading about him winning a couple contests in surf magazines as a grom. As it turned out we were both headed to Jaco. I told him that I had a ride there, and he can tag along if he helps split the fare.

After an hour drive through the jungle, that was more than horrifying because the roads are sometimes one lane, and nobody seems to hit their breaks. The traffic itself seemed to flow together, with me holding the "oh shit" handle the entire time. We stopped only once to see some crocodiles in a river for a few minutes before we made it to Jaco. As we pulled up to the hostel I was booked at, his friend Tyler was staying in the same one. They were shooting some kind of Commercial for the hostel and posting it on social media. This was what they do for a living.

The next day I was to travel to the south of the country chasing a wave called Pavones. It's supposed to be one of the longest lefts in the world. I ended up running into Cory and Tyler on my way to the bus station. They were headed to a spot that required a boat to access. Following my rule of going with the flow, I decided to tag along and help out with the boat Fair. The place was called Playa Escondidos. This was a completely perfect wave breaking over a slab type Reef, that was sharp as hell.

As I promised myself, I would go with the flow. Less than 24 hours off the plane, I had already made some amazing friends, and surfed world class waves. I ended up staying in Jaco a couple of times because that's where I was feeling it. I traveled here and there. Most places I'd go to were beautiful, but I felt the flow of Jaco. As long as I was flowing, there was always something interesting about to happen.

Case and point, I was floating in the pool at the hostel trying to nurse a hangover, when a guy walked by with a surfboard. I asked him how the surf was out front, and he said that he hadn't surfed yet but he was headed to Playa Hermosa. Playa Hermosa was a wave that I grew up drawing on my school folders, it was what you think of when you say a world class beach break in Costa Rica.

The guy I was talking to was from New Zealand. I introduced myself and asked him if I could tag along, he was super stoked to have me join. He was a little disgruntled however, because he had bought a surfboard previously from one of the local shops, and they had rented it out, and now he was riding a beat up loaner board.

As we were loading up our surfboards to go to Playa Hermosa, I grabbed the board I had rented the day before, and it turned out to be the board he bought. Talk about irony. If I would have never said anything to him, I probably would have kept the board all week and he was only there for the night. But instead I ended up surfing world class Playa Hermosa at 5 to 6 feet and he got to have the board he bought. My trip was full of coincidences and instances just like this over and over. The more I would flow the more it would flow to me.

Even the streets were trippy to walk through. There were cars everywhere with motorcycles weaving in and out of traffic. But I noticed that locals would hardly stop before crossing the street on foot. It was interesting to see at first, but after a few days I was right there with them. The trick seemed to be a joke in and of itself, you pretty much walked in a leap of faith into traffic, but somehow managed to be right in the gaps. Like it was all in on it or something... like it flowed.

About my second week I was back in Jaco, I was reflecting on a number of ironic events that have been happening. It was a small 3 to 4 foot day at the local beach break. I checked the surf with a few people, and nobody was feeling the surf but me. I ended up surfing almost 6 hours off and on by myself. It didn't look good from shore, but it was without a doubt, the best day I surfed while I was there.

Costa Rica has a 9ft tide swing, so the locals say to check it every 40 minutes because it will change. I was out the entire day watching it change. I found myself for hours being the only person out. And as I was flowing with my life in Costa Rica, I was flowing with the tide and as it came in. Every wave seemed to get better, after 3 hours I had begun to say one more wave, but they just kept getting better. By the 4th hour I had to eat.

On my last wave riding in to eat, I encountered something that Surfers are all too familiar with. I took off on a 4 foot set and as I bottom turned I flew up and cracked the lip. As I came down, the wave set up for another, and then another, and then another. Before I knew it I was hopping off my surfboard and running onto dry sand on the beach. " How many turns was that?" " "Who the hell was that surfing my board?" These questions pulsing through my mind as I reflected back on a wave that I may have surfed better than any wave I've ever ridden before. One-hit led straight to the other, the next turn blended to the next off the lip, and finally around the roundhouse cutback into the final snap off the top right on the sand. It was almost as if I didn't have to do any work; everything just flowed together.

Right on the beach the locals sell acai bowls, and I decided to grab one. As I ate it on the beach watching the surf, I was in disbelief that there was still nobody out. I stayed out the rest of that day sunburnt and dehydrated. And as I was reflecting on the surf, the town, the whole country. It all seemed to do what I was doing in a harmonious dance of flow.

Tyler paddled out with me for my last session of the day, by then the tide had already gotten on it. I decided not to rub it in his face that the day was full of amazing waves. But as I was sitting in the lineup reflecting on the waves previous, I had an epiphany while surfing. Sometimes I like to call these "surphiphanies." It has finally dawned on me that while searching for the answer I had been seeking, by going on this trip I made a rule for myself to go with the flow. The Epiphany I came up with was the answer that I received. And that answer was about flow.

Everything in life flows like a river of water. In fact, if water doesn't flow it grows stagnant, just as our lives do. If your life does not flow, it may grow stagnant as mine did. But Rejoice because I challenge you to go with the flow and see if it doesn't change. No matter what, as surfers, and as living creatures on this planet, we will all get caught inside from time to time. There will be sets that we have to take on the head. But as long as you don't give up, press on, and just go with the flow, you will eventually make it back out to ride another wave.

CHAPTER 9

I found an answer….a flowstate. Was it a meditation? Prayer? Was it obtained like enlightenment, as in years of patience building? Most religions say that patience is a virtue. Depending on your religious or spiritual background, what practices you've taken part in or any skill you have mastered, patience is always a key player in becoming enveloped and talented in any one area in life. They say and I agree that it takes the average surfer 4 years to actually learn to surf. This is to call themselves a waterman, they must dedicate at least 4 years of consistent practice at least twice a week to really understand the flow state of the ocean.

I can remember the first couple of years being in the water, I would go everyday alone. There were some days that I would spend the day at the beach from 7am to 4pm in the water not catching one wave. I would try like hell over and over until I couldn't move my arms and go home skunked and feeling like a total kook. I never gave up and never surrendered. Eventually, I started having days where I would catch 3 waves, then 5, then 10, until my sessions became about not getting out of the water until I caught a minimum of 10 waves.

The sessions themselves would come in waves. I'd have a skunked friday and then saturday I'd catch so many waves that I would lose count. It was the best of waves, it was the worst of waves. To this day it still feels like whatever is going on in my life can affect my surf sessions….and vice versa for that matter. Like a mental game using the laws of attraction.

To open my eyes and wake up every morning to a new day full of possibilities, I head to the beach at 4am with a reset in my mind. I would notice that the level of stoke would sometimes reflect the session. If I was happy and unassuming and landed on the perfect day of chest high rippable surf, then it just put my day into a flowstate of what seemed like magic. However if I went thinking it was going to be going off, only to find 2ft windy grovely waves or getting caught inside on every head high set… it became frustrating, my day seemed to tailspin into an existence of catching every red light and unwanted traction around every corner.

So there was something to be said about a mental state while riding waves. According to Napoleon Hill's philosophy/ self help book "Think and grow rich", or "The Secret" by Rhonda Byrne, there is a force at work in the universe called "The law of attraction". In this notion or philosophy, our mind controls our reality. If you think in a positive vibration then you begin to vibrate in a harmonious way to attract positive things in your life, if you think negatively, then you attract negative things. It's fairly simple to understand but nearly impossible to apply to everyday life without an incalculable amount of discipline. To achieve a chronic positive state of mind in the world of the 21st century is close to impossible with the stress of the living in the first world. Don't get me wrong, it's a lot more luxurious to live in a place with running water and unlimited food but the chemistry of fear stays the same.

When the brain reacts to stress or fear, it's the same chemical in any situation. When you stress or feel fear, it is a mixture of cortisol and adrenaline that reacts with receptors in your brain to respond to a cognitive response called " fight or flight". This has been a perfect design for survival in the jungles of Africa 10,000 years ago, but does nothing but cause anxiety in the first world. It's a big problem in modern day sosciety because there is no room for a reaction like that when you are not being chased by a lion but you are still having the same reaction when you are stressed about something like money.

When the human body gets stressed out, due to finances, lack of exercise, malnutrition, or loneliness, it begins to break down. Stress is called "the silent killer" of the first world. When you apply this to the "law of attraction" it's like the more you stress, the more your body gives you reasons to stress until it eventually eliminates itself. When the mind is under this much pressure to make money, keep their spouse happy and around, or fulfill the basic needs to survive and be successful in the modern age, all while keeping a positive mental attitude, it seems we are all doomed for failure.

According to the books on " the law of attraction" , there is no judgment when it comes to the law of attraction. Vibration is vibration. If you are stressed or angry, you vibrate at a lower frequency than if you are happy or positive which vibrates high. Vibration and frequency in itself are just waves of energy. Nicola Tesla once said "If you want to find the secrets of the universe, think in terms of energy, frequency and vibration." Energy, frequency, and vibration are all ways of measuring waves.

To get to a state of mind where one is the antenna sending and receiving positive frequencies, you must first vibrate at the right level of energy to match it. This I believe is where every religion on the planet says that patience comes to play. Whether it be a type of meditation, or prayer, I believe that it's all a practice in patience. To pray is to meditate on something you desire or are thankful for what is already in the happening. According to understanding the laws, "to believe is to receive". So to pray and have faith is to already have it. It's said to always have faith in every religion. And what is faith if not just thinking about what you want positively?

So how does one obtain the state to be at a positive mindset all the time? There's numerous books and gurus that make millions a year just to answer this very question. People write books and books on this subject in so many different avenues to achieve this that its hard to see what is true from false. After combing for years through every self help and religious section this side of the galaxy, I had begun to see a pattern in the similarities of the philosophy.

-In the bible, Jesus says "With faith the size of a mustard seed you can move a mountain." Mathew 17:20

-"So lose not heart nor fall into despair, for you will be superior if you are true in faith" Qur'an -3:139

-"How very little can be done under the spirit of fear" -Florence Nightingale

-" If you do not see riches in your imagination, you will not see them in your bank account." - Napoleon Hill

-"Every thought of yours is a real thing....a force." -The Secret

The list goes on and on about your mind being the most powerful tool you have on your side if you train yourself to think correctly. Or your worst enemy if you don't. I can talk from experience about the power of the mind in a flowstate. To me a flow state is when you let go of trying to control your mind and you just let it do what it is designed to do, which is think. When I say let it think, I don't mean the way you try to remember who sang that song, or where you got that painting. The human interaction with the main part of the body that is responsible for all thought functions without you controlling it, the brain.

"The brain...a great servant....a terrible master"- Robin S. Sharma

If you try to control the wave you ride, you're in for a session full of wipeouts. The same is for the brain. For example, while writing this sentence I do it without thought. I simply have faith that I have something to share, have done the research, and now letting my subconscious take over and write it. It's a flow state or I don't even begin the day of writing. The same principal goes for anything in life, especially action sports like surfing.

How many times have you heard the same old story about the athlete that was "in the zone." ? Most champions will admit that while training an ungodly amount in practice, when the moments that mattered appeared during the most important times of the game, match, or competition, that it was in slow motion and almost easy. It's been described in a way where the athlete says " When in that zone, there is no error, you just can't lose." What gets us to that state of mind? And how can we tap into the zone of the brain that connects us to the "flow state."? Is it eating wheaties? Is it faith? Practice? What if the answer was to just not think about it?

If being positive and having faith is the answer, then not thinking about it would be the way. Does a stream have to think to flow? Or does it just be as it is? When it is described by people, and from my own experience, getting to this superhuman-like area in the mind is mostly by having your head right, a positive mindset, practice in the craft, and a dose of magic. The reason that I say magic is because we still can't figure out how people click into it or how it works but it just does.

I don't know if i can speak for everyone, but my best moods come from a good surf. I get out of the water and I just seem more courteous, more relaxed, just better all around. Even if surfing did just this for me, I'd be eternally grateful. The fact that it puts me into a positive mood and allows me to flow through the rest of the aspects of my life make it that bit of magic that i'm looking for in life.

I've been in several flow states in my time on this planet, and all of them have been either during surfing or on a day where I had a good session in the water. Like the sets that we wait for in the line up at your local spot, it seems to come in waves. It comes in the days when the elements all come together, the stars align, and my mindset is positive. To me the point of life is to find this state and I find it in the water. The way is faith and positivity, and i recieve that from being in the ocean, just doing what I love. Flowing with water.

CHAPTER 10

Most people, when they think of surfing, Might think of Jeff Spicoli from Fast Times at Ridgemont High. A long haired, hippie stoner, half educated with no job. Hollywood does a good job at characterizing the "sport" or lifestyle that has such a deep meaning to the people that do it, that they are misunderstood by people who view it from the outside looking in.

This view is common in human nature to anybody that doesn't understand something that's out of their comfortable bubble that they inhabit themselves in. For instance, if somebody has never been to church their entire adult life, it might seem very strange to them. To see people singing together to something that none of them can see, and bowing their heads to pray to a force they've never spoken to might be strange. To this person, they may walk out of church thinking the people inside need to seek help mentally. But to the people who are in the church, they live a faith-based life of servitude towards a higher power, usually responsible for intelligent design of all things. Again, to a person who doesn't understand, it all might seem very strange.

This is a common theme in the United States, the land of freedom where one is free to do what he pleases and everybody usually does. At times it can even divide us because of misunderstanding each other. For example, metalheads and Yogi's usually aren't the best of friends, in the same way that Catholics and Jehovah's Witnesses aren't usually seen talking to one another because their philosophies are different.

My Philosophy put into words, is simply this: Surfers are misunderstood by everybody else because surfing itself as a lifestyle is only understood by those who do it. In my eyes surfing is a religion.

What makes a good religion? First and foremost, for an argument to be made that surfing is a true religion, it would have to have some type of fellowship following, a philosophy, a holy land or Mecca, rules and controversy, a deep understood history, leaders of the movement, and last but not least some type of mosque or sanctuary.

The ancient Hawaiians have a written history of Surfing that goes back 1600 years. They had an entire religion based around it. So this is no original idea, just one that I'm defending and resurfacing for those who feel the same way. Now there is no church of Surfing that I'm aware of, however there is a sanctuary littered with people from all walks of life. A sanctuary so sacred that people are fighting to protect it and some go just to enjoy its beauty. Our sanctuary is the ocean.

It's pretty much universally agreed on that the ocean, in most places, may just be the most beautiful place to be on earth. People travel far and wide to many different beaches around the world to bask in its beauty. From the beaches of California to the Bungalow Villas of Bora Bora. There is an industry of people who make a living just taking pictures of the ocean for people to put up and their cubicles at work. These photographs are usually there to gaze upon while waiting for their vacation hours to rack up so they could spend a week sipping drinks with umbrellas on a beach with white sand and blue water in some far off destination. From regular vacationers to sailors, to Surfers and bodyboarders, many agree that the ocean is the biggest sanctuary of all.

Just as the eskimos have hundreds of words for different snow and ice conditions, so too do the Hawaiians have just as many words to explain the ocean and it's conditions. Their history and mythology is loaded with taboos and rituals, all based on riding waves and sailing seas. An interesting taboo that sticks out in the ancient Hawaiian hierarchy of surfing, was that the King's royal family were able to take whatever waves they wanted, and if a peasant had the nerve to drop in on their wave, by ancient Hawaiian law the king was allowed to take him to shore and kill him. Surfing to the ancient Hawaiians was religion not taken lightly.

In some places around the world, this is still practiced on a milder scale called "localism". If you were to just paddle out at a new surf break, there's a chance that the local guys may throw you a beating. It's not like this everywhere but there are definitely places like pipeline, J-bay, or even Palos Verdes California that's known to still uphold a type of Surfing hierarchy. These territorial locals are surfing's warriors of controversy, and they take it very seriously.

As for elders in our church of surfing, we have both Legends of the sport, and guru's of its lifestyle. Duke Kahanamoku is the modern day Abraham of surfing. In this sense, he spread the sport globally from Hawaii to Australia to the US. He would do demonstrations in the early nineteen-hundreds. Duke, was an Olympic swimmer and most known in the world of surfing as its biggest Guru and highest ranked Legend.

After Duke Kahanamoku spread the sport or lifestyle, there became an almost deadhead style following that erupted in its wake. When I say deadhead Style, I mean about the band The Grateful Dead who had toured the United States in the sixties and seventies and still into today. With this band came a following of people who gave up regular life and followed the group to every stop on their tour. They made a living by selling handmade trinkets on blankets outside the shows, only making enough to get in the show, eat, and get to the next destination. These followers became known as "Deadheads".

The early days of surfing in the fifties and sixties definitely had their share of deadhead look-alikes. Once they discovered how much fun you could have surfing, everything else seemed to go out the window. I'm under a belief that they found the spiritual side of Surfing and a type of Zen not found anywhere else in "society". Some gave up everything they owned to live in the sanctuary of the beach, and live the lifestyle of a "Surf bum" (a term used by people who didn't understand what it was that attracted these people to poverty and how they seem so happy about it.)

In most religions, they involve some type of pilgrimage. For Mormons when they are of age they have to spend two years as missionaries for the Mormon church. I'm sure you've seen them riding their bikes around in their suits and ties and most likely had knocked on your door at one point. This is just a pilgrimage that is required by the religion to further their spiritual walk. It is the same in the Muslim faith that every person of this religion has to make it to Mecca one day to circled the Holy Temple and place their hand on the holy Stone. In the religion of surfing there's many different types of pilgrimages.

In 1966 a surfer by the name of Bruce Brown made a film called the Endless Summer. The film was about two Surfers who Venture off into the unknown of the world looking for the Endless Summer full unridden waves and new surf spots. Until this film was made, most people only surfed in Hawaii, California, Australia and South Africa. And most Surfers were territorial and rarely left their home brakes.

The post Endless Summer era gave way to something that most Surfers hold dear to their hearts "THE SURF TRIP". This led to the expansion of Surfing to pretty much every continent in the world. In this day and age, in the 21st century, people search almost anywhere water touches land, even in the Great Lakes. In this day and age, no Surfer is truly complete without some type of adventure into the unknown to surf waves he's heard about, in a country he doesn't speak the language of. All part of the adventure but not quite the pilgrimage.

Just as the Muslims have to travel to Mecca for their true pilgrimage and their Holy Land, so too do surfers have to travel to their Holy Land of Hawaii. The North Shore of Oahu is considered the Seven Mile miracle, the Israel or Mecca of surfing. To be a complete Surfer, one should visit the Holy Land, respect the locals, and surf the North Shore of Oahu. This is a place where you will learn respect for the ocean, humility from the locals, and most of all you will be tested to your limits of what you can actually handle on the ocean.

My first pilgrimage to Oahu I did by myself. I landed in Honolulu With a backpack and no plan (In my true fashion) but to surf the North Shore. I ended up staying with a buddy of mine in Honolulu for a few days, which his girlfriend was a bit uptight and less than thrilled to have me stay with them as I covered a couple chapters ago.

The first few days in the North Shore were pretty minimal. There was talk of a swell coming in a few days, but to me it was plenty of surf in November on the North Shore. I surfed all over the place from Pipeline, to Rocky Point, even the Waimea shorebreak. But what I didn't know was that to the locals these were flat days.

I remember reading that the North Shore was getting swell soon. That day came, and it looked really fun at 6 to 8 ft with some kind of scary plus size in between. I decided to paddle out at Rocky lefts because it had a decent Channel and I'm a goofy foot so I wanted to be on my forehand in waves the size. After catching four or five waves, I noticed I kept having a paddle out a little bit further each time. Within an hour of my surf, I went from confidently surfing in six to eight foot fun waves, to scared wet cat status, as 15-20ft sets began pouring through. This was the largest surf I'd ever been out in and I was stuck in it.

After about 30 minutes of fighting for my life through the treacherous currents on my 6-foot board, my arms were noodles. It took me another 15 minutes to just rest and get pushed through the area through gas Chambers, I finally mustered up the courage to take off on an in-between set. Lucky for me, a 12 foot between set came and washed me through to the inside. As I stood on shore gasping for air, I realized that I had been put to the test and I found my limit. I think this is something every Surfer must go through on a spiritual surfing Journey, to the Mecca of the Northshore.

I guess in a way I felt blessed. To know my limits, to be tested past them, and come out the other side alive, was in itself one of the most spiritual experiences I've ever had. The next day the sun felt a little warmer, the food tasted that much better, and my respect & humbleness levels were at an all-time high.

Just paddling out into the ocean of the unknown can be considered a faith-based choice. The fact that you can drown at any moment, get eaten by a shark, have a zen or spiritual experience, or possibly have the ride of your life, is in itself, some type of Russian Roulette style coin toss. The odds of a shark attack or drowning are very rare, but you do hear about it from time to time because they do happen.

I once stayed on Big Island for a month in Hawaii surfing banyans. They were rumors of sharks in every direction. I kept hearing about a great white that was lurking around the area and every time I paddled out, it felt kind of eerie. About four days after I got back on the plane to the mainland, a guy got his arm bitten by a great white at the very spot that I was surfing every day. So the Russian roulette is very real at times. But the faith must remain.

Our faith is based on the moment that you will have some type of spiritual Zen like experience on the ride of your life from time to time. It's what keeps us paddling out past fins and into the food chain, panicking on a bad wipeout, dealing with sunburnt skin, and closeouts on the head. Like a drug addict constantly chasing his high, we constantly search for that moment. It's a religious experience not found in a temple, but in a sanctuary. The ocean is the Sanctuary for us that surf. It is here that no matter how many times it tries to kill you, and no matter how many times it almost has, with faith we focus only on the times it makes us feel alive.

CHAPTER 11

If I was to Proclaim surfing as its own religion, then I would easily say that not only is it the best one, but the healthiest as well. If you were to approach a Wellness Health coach and ask for the formula of Health, I believe that you would most likely get the same answer from anyone that you ask. Watch your diet, get plenty of exercise and sunshine, be social, have a type of prayer, yoga, or meditation. Also, spend a lot of time in nature and less in front of the television set.

I know most children surfers in Southern California prefer to have a mexican burrito or a cheeseburger after a long surf session. But, I have noticed the average surfer from anywhere that begins to reach their mid-to-late twenties, tends to become more involved with what goes in their bodies. Especially today, in the age of information and Kelly Slater. I say Kelly Slater because he brought the health food movement to the sport of Surfing and put it in the public eye. Nobody knew how he could surf into his 50s and compete against the guys on the world tour in their late teens and early twenties and kick their ass. But his Elixir to life is extremely public and more so simpler. Kelly Slater claims his longevity as diet being the biggest Factor. You are what you eat and you surf what you eat too.

It's no secret that diet is an important factor in any person's life no matter if they're an athlete surfer or a nine-to-five cubicle worker. Hippocrates said " let thy food be thy medicine. " and since Kelly Slater and the top Surfers in the world began to write books to unleash their secrets of longevity, health and diet have been at the very top of the lists for most of these Surfers. There's been an enormous food-based Health Trend in the sport of surfing. To keep up with the extreme physical demand that surfing requires, you have to put the right fuel in your body.

I've read that the best thing to eat before surfing is nothing. Most of the pros will drink a bunch of water, sometimes with lemon in it as a pre-surf beverage. But after a good surf session, or any athletic activities, it's all about the recovery. If you wanted to ride waves into your 80s like Doc Paskowits, then putting the right food into your body is the way.

In most religions, there are dietary restrictions. If I'm going to make an argument about surfing as a religion, I would say there has to be some type of rule about keeping the temple of your body clean. I'm not saying to become a vegan, I'm simply stating that if you want to surf for the rest of your life, maybe fast food is not the best choice for that goal. I encourage people to clean up their diet and watch their surfing and mental states begin to peek.

The next thing about the religion of Surfing that is so beneficial, would be the exercise. The average person in a first-world country doesn't get nearly enough exercise. This is due to all the comforts of living in a society that sits down at work, sits down to drive home, sits down to travel, sits down to watch TV, and sits down just to relax at the end of the day.

Some Studies have shown that surfing can burn up to 250 calories an hour on average. This is the equivalent of running two and a half miles. If you surf everyday for one week, and some people do surf everyday, it's the equivalent two running 17 and a half miles in 1 week.

This isn't even mentioning the fact that half of the time, Surfers have to hold their breath and learn how to relax in a situation that at times, can feel like you're about to die. I can hold my breath for about a minute-and-a-half, this turns into about 10 seconds on a bad wipeout. After paddling, duck diving, and finally surfing which is an exercise in itself, if you happen to fall, you still go for a ride that the wave takes you on under the water while holding your breath. After a while, your body begins building an endurance that can only be rivaled by soccer players.

My Uncle Mike used to surf, but then he said he had to give it up because it was entirely too much exercise for him. " All that paddling for the itty bitty ride." He'd say. Of course, there is no choice for the surfer that has been hooked on the sport. For the surfer who tries to paddle out as often as possible, has to stay in shape if they want to continue to ride waves. Thus far, unaware of any other religion in which you have to stay in shape and healthy for.

If you've ever owned a dog or a cat, you would notice that even if they were an inside animal, during the middle of the day they would find an area in the house that the sun shines in and lay in it for a couple of hours a day. The indigenous people of the United States, when asked how they learned how to survive and what to eat, they said "Watch the animals.... eat what they eat....do as they do." I think it's interesting that the Instinct of any animal is to get plenty of sunshine. Us humans have to be told that it's good for us in order for us to make time to lay out and catch some rays.

Although it's against every beauty tip in the book, it is scientifically proven that sunlight is one of the healthiest things you can do for yourself that costs no money. Too much of it and skin damage begins to occur, sometimes resulting in skin cancer, not enough sunshine and you begin to become vitamin D deficient. There's a balance to be had when dealing with the sun, especially in summer time. Every Surfer knows the pain of when the waves get good and the water warm, they'd be dealing with sunburnt backs and cherry red faces.

However, the rest of the world may not be getting enough sunlight, but Surfers are forced into it. The only shade we get is if we pull into a good-sized barrel. With tan skin and Sun bleached hair, I'd say that most Surfers that are not surfing in the Arctic Circle are getting a sufficient amount of sunlight per day. It's not rocket science to know that it's good for you but it is scientifically proven that it's extremely beneficial for humans to bask in the sun in moderation.

Along with sunlight would be the fact that not enough people in modern society spent enough time in nature. When people think of nature they think of the Woods, grasslands, or camping in the mountains. But the ocean is nature that is in fact out of our element. Some of the happiest people in the world say the secret to their happiness is spending time in nature. The love of surfing Demands that we climb off the land and into the sea where there are animals such as dolphins and sharks. Where there is no scoreboard or deadlines. It's as a sailor would say "Just you and the ocean." This is a sport where you are truly In God's playground.

There is a theory about people who stay in nature a lot, that's not just about the peace and tranquility of the experience itself. Mystics have said that people who walk barefoot on the earth receive the vibration of it as a living Organism. Or others have claimed that it releases the negative ions from your spine and "grounds out" your nervous system.

Whether these claims are true or not, or if it can be measured by some type of Scientific instruments, the fact is, Surfers generally walk on the sand without shoes, and surf in the water with their bare feet. Perhaps surfers have been grounded by this method and never even meant to, and no it's not scientifically proven, but It's still a fun thought, and a serious belief for some people.

The benefits are endless when it comes to being in the ocean. It's scientifically proven stat about always being an ocean water, would be the levels of magnesium in your system. Most people, when they have a tough day, like to relax in an Epsom salt bath. This release is magnesium through the skin into the body, having a very relaxed effect. If you serve in the ocean every day, you too will Absorb this beneficial element.

The next amazing benefits in the religion of surfing, would be the social aspect. Unless you're surfing on a Saturday at lower trestles, generally most of the lineups are pretty friendly. It's been said that a lot of religions, especially the Christian religion has found a support group in the fellowship of their church. Having some form of fellowship is amazingly beneficial for the psyche of your average human being. It gives the feeling of belonging, being wanted, helping others, and being social.

Most of my social life where I talk to people about real issues that generally don't have to do with work or Sports have been in the water. In a way, the group of surfers that I grew up with, that I still surf with today have been a support group of people that no matter what's going on in their life, I can always find them on a 5-foot offshore day at our local spot. I've had friends come and go throughout my life but the surfing ones have always stayed, because even if we grow distant we still meet up at least once a week for church in the water.

In a way it's like a family. When you meet somebody and find out they are a surfer I tend to look at them differently. Or if you're a surfer, and you paddle out there's always somebody that you can relate with to talk to in the water. The old guys on longboards at Bolsa Chica will tell you stories of the past swells and places they surfed, the rippers will always be bumping elbows with everybody, and all of us will be helping out the 3-foot groms in the shorebreak.

I've had old Surfers be my mentors, locals kick me out of the water, and saved by strangers when things weren't going my way. I've had Surfers my age be my challenge and even fight me sometimes in the water. I've helped little groms when they get in a sticky situation on a big day. We do this cuz we've all been that Grom, and one day we'll all be that old guy. It's like a family of people around the world, we're all part of the same tribe, the same religion of surfing.

And as in any religion there has to be some type of prayer or meditation. I believe every Surfer that has been out on anything over 6 feet of a day , has begun to say prayers when the cleanup sets come through. But on a serious note, surfing has been described as one of the most Zen-like forms of Lifestyle next to Buddhism. Staring into the ocean, waiting for that perfect wave can sometimes be a test of patience and in a way... ...a meditation.

Not to mention, what I have come to call "the art relaxation" As a surfer you have to learn to relax in various situations that at times can seem like life or death. When cleanup sets come through, you have to relax in order to keep your heart rate down and your muscles from burning all the oxygen you have.

Same goes in a bad wipeout on a larger wave. Personally, on a wipeout that's tearing me apart and holding me under the water , I go to a place in my head that's far from the ocean like a waterfall or garden. Pretty much anything to keep my mind off the fact that I'm being thrown like a rag doll and in a dog's mouth underwater, and there's nothing I can do until it lets me go. This frame of mind that I go into in these hairy situations, I would call a type of meditation. I feel that's what caused the stereotype of a surfer in Hollywood to be so calm, cool and relaxed on land, almosted "stoned" because they are forced to learn to stay relaxed in violent situations while in the water.

Along with cleaning up your eating habits, for performance surfing, you have to also have flexible muscles. Yoga or stretching can help you to deal with the endurance required to survive bad wipeouts on oversized days. A lot of surfers and professionals have resorted to such practices like yoga and pilates for strength training, flexibility, and balance. Yoga in itself has been referred to as a religion at times. It's quite the challenge full of benefits mentally and physically for a surfers lifestyle.

Another beautiful aspect of surfing is that it taps into a primal operation in the mind. Ask a surfer, any real Surfer about his best wave and he'll have a legend to tell. We are all descended from warriors, soldiers, and pioneers of the world. In the 21st century there are many ways to get your thrill. Some people jump out of airplanes, others do drugs. But if you catch a surfer on a 6-8ft day with A-frame Peaks, and offshore winds, the chances are,adrenaline is pumping through his veins and his heart is beating out of his chest. They know it's about to be one of those sessions. And generally if they do have one of those sessions, they will never forget it.

The risk is worth the reward paddling out past fins and into the food chain just for one more wave. And for some people it gives them a reason to go on, a reason to stay healthy, even for some people it's the only reason to live. For somebody who just had the session of their life, it can feel like you just won a fight, or the big game. You have tapped into that primal nature while dancing with the force of a storm that created a wave, traveled halfway across the world for you to tap into that energy of, and have a near life experience to satisfy your Primal instincts.

This lifestyle without a doubt is the most religious feeling I've ever had, and the closest whatever you call God that I've ever experienced.

CHAPTER 12

Just like in any religion there's going to be times where you lose faith and stray off. Surfing has a way of teaching you lessons the way life does. In a religious faith, people can be so immersed that the world just passes them by and nothing else seems to matter. It becomes their addiction for addiction, usually to overcome addiction.

In AA meetings one of the first things you have to do in a 12 step program, is surrender to a higher power in order to beat your addiction. On my trip to Costa Rica I remember being in the taxi with Cory . As we talked about surfing, I told him about this book that I was writing about surfing as a religion and the only way of life. We discussed a lot, but one thing that stuck was the story about a woman who was addicted to heroin and had to give up all her friends to stray from the drugs. She then also had to move away from her home, and the only thing that kept her on track was surfing. It was her own way to surrender to some type of higher power.

Now I don't know this lady's story, but I can tell you that in addiction, you can fall back. And just like any addiction, including the cure to addiction, is sometimes just another, more healthy addiction to fall back too. Surfing might be one of the greatest things a human can do in your life. It can bring you to the other side, and understand what is truly meaningful. It can fulfill your life like no drug or person ever will. But there are going to be times in your life whether you know it or not, where it becomes obsolete. I know this because it happened to me

My father was an extremely religious man. Since I fell away from the church and the faith that he believes in so deeply, he used to try to get me back to a faith that I just can't see anymore. My new religion became surfing. It became my Foundation for faith that I found tangible. But I wrote this chapter in a time where I drive to the beach with my surfboard & my wetsuit, and I stare at the waves and they have zero appeal to me.

I can't count the times I've watched perfect waves break, shrugged my shoulders and left the beach. I've done it several times, almost in a jaded form. I worked my entire life to live next to the beach so that I could surf everyday and build the foundation of my way of life as a surfer. The funny part is, once I had achieved this... surfing began to stray.

I don't know whether I lost faith or if it's just a part of being Surfer to go back in life and evaluate everything including your foundation. But as I sat there reading these words, looking at the palm tree that indicates the wind for me, the wind is offshore and I know for a fact the waves are good but I can't face the ocean. I'm not sure if it's some type of neglect or loss of faith because this was the first time something like this has happened to me. The problem was that it had been going on like this all year.

The strangest part of it all, is that it came at a time when I was truly at the peak of my surfing. I know this because I've been doing contests my whole life, and it came at a time when I won my first contest and took the entire series. I was 28, a time when most Surfers retire. And shortly thereafter I felt accomplished, but I also felt like I was surfing for the wrong reasons. This isn't to say that contests are bad, but the state of mind it can put you into, I think can be.

When I was training for a contest it was always fun because I was surfing, but once I'd begun to win, that's all that became important to me. Every time I went surfing with my friends, they would snort like a pig because I was being a wave hog. Almost to the point where nobody wanted to Surf with me anymore. I wasn't doing it with soul, I wasn't doing it with love, I wasn't doing it for the right reasons. And I believe because of this, I lost the drive.

What is it that drives us to get up at 6 a.m. everyday, climb into some rubber, and jump in the freezing cold ocean? For me when I was doing it for the right reasons, I hardly noticed how cold it was, I hardly noticed the crowd in the lineup, I hardly noticed it was something that people do every day on the regular. For me, it was just the way life was. It was my way to see God in her true beauty. It was my way of tapping into the source.

Once again, contests are not bad, I love watching them. They're one of my favorite things to do or watch. But if you're doing this for the wrong reasons, you can fall short of the glory, especially if you win. The same can be said about a career choice you take that might leave you inland. The same can be said about a girl or a boy that you choose to spend time with instead of tapping into the source. The same thing can be said about an addiction you may have. It doesn't have to be something that necessarily takes you away from the ocean. For me, it was one that immersed me into the ocean but took me away from the soul of everything that gave me the light of love that I acquired in the beginning.

The beach giveth and the beach taketh away. I wasn't sure what to do since I lost my drive to the ocean. "What do you do when your foundation crumbles? That's something they don't teach in schools." (Slc punk) I think the right answer is the same you would get in an Alcoholics Anonymous meeting. First you have to admit that there's a problem. Mine was that I was surfing for all the wrong reasons.

And some might think that it's a silly way to look at it, but what is it that was keeping me away? How was it I had fallen short? Is it a girl? Was it a job? Was it an addiction? Surfing for the wrong reasons? Whatever it was, understand that in times when surfing cannot be achieved, when you lost your drive to go visit your mother ocean, this is the time to go inward.

I have said it before and I'll continue to say, in every surf session, there's one wave that makes the entire session. And in every Surfers life there's one session and makes the Surfers life. By keeping the drive, you have to understand the fact that this session has not come yet...not until your last session. By Keeping the drive... the stoke... the faith... you believe that the best session of your life is yet to come.

That's what keeps us coming back to the beach, spending all their money on surfboards, and dealing with severe hypothermia, just to see if this next session it's going to be the one we're chasing. No matter what happens, realize that surfing is a religion, and just like any religion, you have to keep the faith. Believe that your best wave, your best surf session has yet to come. Believe in the good waves coming!

Be patient and understanding when the ocean doesn't call to you. It's a hard thing to understand and a big lesson to learn. Having faith just like any religion is necessary in this one. There will be times of trials and tribulations for every Surfer. It's just up to you to weather this storm. Keep the faith my brothers and sisters, because there will be times the ocean doesn't call to you for reasons you can't understand. These are important times to pay attention to. Focus inwardly and listen.

Remember that there's always another wave, there's always another time that you will be stoked as long as you keep the ocean in your heart and close. Because through these times, we will truly see what type of surfers we are.

There's some of these times I've known people that quit altogether and moved inland. I've even done it myself. I've seen them not surf for 20 years and then come back to the ocean and have the best session they've ever had in their entire life.

My uncle Frosty was one of the most avid Surfers I've ever seen. But when he had kids and moved inland for years and years. But every time he comes out to California, he borrows one of my boards and paddles out. It may not be the way he remembers it when he was doing it everyday, but I can tell you as a witness, when I see him catch a good one, he reminds me of my first wave every time. The Stoke is truly untouchable.

It was his stoke that had originally got me in the water. Some of my first memories are of the beach. My uncle Frosty took me to Trestles on a camping trip where he surfed his guts out. One of my first memories was standing on shore and watching him. I knew then that I was going to surf.

Life has a way of throwing curve balls at us for reasons that at the time it's completely unknown. If surfing is your religion, the way it's my religion, have faith and just wait. Even the best surf session has lulls between the sets. So if you're at a time in your life where surfing isn't appealing or the ocean is not calling, just understand that it's just a lull, just a break, just a pause in between the sets of your sessions. Keep the faith, because she's going to call you back one day, so you better be ready.

CHAPTER 13

Upon getting back from Costa Rica, my life was changed forever. First of all, the only thing I kept thinking the entire time I was down there was "Where else would I be if not here? " What I mean by this, is that if I had not changed my life path, quit my job, and bought a random ticket to Central America, I would not have had one of the most life-changing experiences I could possibly imagine.

How far was I willing to take this? If there's one thing that rings true, it's that we have one life to live that we are aware of. Anything that comes afterwards to me, almost seems like what came before. I don't remember anything before I was born, I wonder if I'll know anything after I die?

The only thing that I know for sure, is that right now, I have breath in my lungs and my heart is still pumping. I also know that if there's one thing that's guaranteed in life…it's death. I always remember this during times of bad luck when suicide runs its selfish thoughts through my mind. Anytime I get into that mindset, I just remember one thing... we are all going to the grave, it doesn't matter how rich you are, how healthy you are, and it doesn't matter what you know, all of us will end up there given a long enough timeline. So why be in a hurry to get there?

So with that knowledge, why would we live such Mundane lives? Why would we only focus on relaxing when we're old and decrepit? Why not live a life worth dying for? It was thoughts like these that would not let me go back to a regular job.

It was thoughts like these that made me analyze life differently. The more I realized that I only have one life to live, the sweeter everything began to taste. And surfing waves began to be the only thing that made sense to me. People say that having kids is without a doubt the reason we are here. But why are they here? To have more kids?

The only thing that I truly began to understand, was when I looked at life as a limited number of days, I wanted to fill all those days with fun. I wanted to fill all those days with surfing. Maybe one day I will have kids and understand that side of life, but for now, what brings me peace is the ocean. And that's all I really needed to understand.

After a couple months of working odd jobs and doing some traveling, I ended up going to burningman at the last-second on a whim. I had decided to go the night before everybody left. It was life-changing. I had been there before, but this time was much different. I spent a lot of time on psychedelics and with King philosophers on the playa.

I can tell you everything that happened both mystical and strange, but that would be an entirely different book. The philosophy I took from this trip was that I had one life to live and I was going to do it differently from now on. One day I will die, so why get caught in a loop of monotony.

I got addicted to traveling up and down the coast of California, surfing waves and festival hopping. I had found a few odd ways to make money, like being an Uber driver with a surfboard on top of my car. At this time, you could actually drive into San Francisco and get up every day at four in the morning to take everyone to work. I was making almost 2 grand- a week doing this. You definitely earned the money because it's a highly stressful situation at that time in the morning in the city.

I ended up outside of San Francisco that September at a music festival called symbiosis. I was meeting up with the people that I had met at burningman. It was a wonderful time and I was convinced to stay the day after the festival by my friend Simba. We ended up eating psychedelics and swimming with a bunch of naked people. And that's when Simba and I decided to make a different plan.

Instead of driving back to Southern California, we ended up driving north into Humboldt County. We landed jobs as weed trimmers for the marijuana industry. We stayed with our friend Tony who we called "Baby Grandpa". One of the most mysterious and influential people I've ever met in my life.

It was here I didn't surf much. There was a beach, but the conditions were ice cold, it was always foggy, and not to mention the waters are entirely shark infested. Most of the good surf spots were taken by the real locals, seals everywhere in the lineup. I went to check the surf one day and it actually looked fun, but the fog rolled in, so instead I went and had a beer at the Local brewery. On the wall was a surfboard with a giant bite taken out of it. Turns out a local wasn't so lucky.

Most of my time in this area was spent on psychedelics, working on trim scenes, and meeting people from all over the world. It was here that I discovered a different type of flow. There were people on these trim scenes that did not surf, but they traveled and lived a life worth living. Most of them were from very humble means and never had much money to speak of. But all of them full of life.

It was one of the first times I could actually relate with somebody who didn't surf. Of course when you talk to them, they said that they were surfing the waves of life. The stoke they felt was riding one wave at a time of positive energy. It sounds like hippie stuff, but most of it comes from eastern philosophy.

A lot of the surfing world was influenced by eastern philosophy in the 1960s. As was the American culture. There were gurus and teachers that came out of India and influenced the hippie culture, which in turn influenced the surf culture that seems to go hand in hand. People who were forced to read the Bible as a kid were now reading the Bhagavad-Gita and learning about Lord Krishna instead of Jesus Christ.

I can admit that I fell into this trend in the hippie community as well. But as a kid who grew up reading the Bible, when I read the Bhagavad-Gita, I felt like I was reading a different story with the same message. That message was encapsulated and projected in the 50s and 60s by music culture as well.

"All you need is love!" As it was said Best by the Beatles. I saw a picture once, of Jesus Christ, Krishna, Lord Ganesh, and an array of the world's religious Messiahs Standing behind the DJ booth. The caption read "Same song, different DJ." When you collaborate eastern and western philosophies, you come to the same conclusion as the Beatles. The same conclusion as the hippie community which is "peace and love. "

I was in Humboldt for four months at this time, I lived with hippies, I worked with travelers, tramps, and nomads. And what I found was that the wisest people I've ever met really had nothing and lived in god's good humor. What I mean by this is they just took the leap of faith into life and grew their wings on the way down.

That same spirit that the Australians that I met in Hawaii were living off the "stoke" was everywhere in this community of seemingly homeless people. Of course they did not see themselves as homeless, "home free" was the term I kept running across.

I made a documentary and put it up on YouTube about my adventure up there. It's simply Titled "Humboldt Trim scene documentary" . It pretty much shows everything that I was doing while I was there. Although I was not surfing, I learned a lot about flow states as a way of life.

Flow states as a way of life? I thought Flow states were only in action sports. What if I could combine the two? What if God and vibration were the same thing? What if psychedelics were a key to seeing the truth? These were questions that arose from my adventure. I knew that going home, I was never going to be the same.

The only constant is change, after four months I packed up my truck and drove back south to my apartment in Huntington Beach. My roommate Vinny was more than stoked to see me home. He said it had been depressing without me. But little did he know my adventure had just started. I had to explore this flow state. I had to explore the waves of life. If I was to stay in Huntington Beach and just keep paying rent until I die, then I believe my life would've been wasted.

While sitting on these trim scenes everybody had stories from all over the world. Traveling through Central and South America, traveling through Southeast Asia, traveling everywhere. Their lives were so rich with experience. And the surfers that I met on the trim scenes, had surfed all the waves that I grew up looking at in magazines.

After understanding that I didn't have to pay rent and die, my life has completely changed. When I got back to Huntington Beach, I spent the next three months packing up my stuff. I'm getting ready to go.... somewhere.... I didn't know where. But I had to get there.

To be honest I didn't feel like I was actually going to reach a destination, it felt like the adventure was all in the journey. I could not even hold a conversation with a regular person from southern California anymore. The only thing they could talk about was Netflix, sports, and politics. I was more interested in what was going on and far off Third World countries where waves were breaking without me. I could not waste my time on mundane things that didn't matter. I had to go and taste life.

Of course what was life? Was it a series of flow states? Was it a series of vibrations? How was I going to tap into this thing that everybody called their "flow" ? From what I understand, you just have to go and it starts happening. "Like flowing water" as Bruce Lee said. The flow state can only be achieved by flowing. If water stays still it becomes stagnant. Like most people's lives and they don't even know it, they are a fish, living in a pond, content with that pond instead of swimming down the stream that is accessible to every single fish in this pond.

Surfing became my religion because I discovered a flow state within the sport. Now I am beginning to discover a flow state within life. If I were to discover a way to blend the two, then I feel I would discover the secrets of the universe. But what is the universe? Was it just an accident? Or was it "The big bang" that turned into "the big flow"?

Was all of this an accident? Or is the flow state proof of intelligent design? When I surf and ride that vibration into a flow state, am I communicating with what people call God? Was I discovering the "secrets of the universe"?.

CHAPTER 14

According to science, "in the beginning" there was a random act of an explosion that created the cosmos called the "Big Bang theory". Terence McKenna, when asked about the big bang theory, was quoted as saying "This is a scientific way of saying to religion, to Just give us one miracle, and we'll fill in the blanks." This theory, always seen as a giant collaboration of particles and gasses that came together after a disturbance over eons of years. The particles have found each other with just the right mixture to eventually sustain life.

It is through the birth and death of stars with different foundations for their construction. In the end, eventually becoming a supernova or death of a star in which the life cycle is finished and it collapses into itself. It then explodes in a miniature version of the Big Bang itself. And then sends it's specific elements blasting into the vastness of space. New stars are then born creating their own gravity fields. As these particles pass through them, they get sucked in or begin to orbit the star's gravitational field.

According to modern science, over billions of years the star matures and denses creating more force for the orbiting elements to collect, and eventually become planets. Smaller particles become moons and eventually a solar system is born.

In the Milky Way galaxy, there is an incalculable number of stars orbiting an unknown center and in the universe there is another incalculable number of galaxies, some 100 times the size of our own. The Milky Way is our solar system, and in our solar system is another incalculable number of solid liquid and gas elements orbiting our vast star we know as the sun.

The collection makes eight (nine) planets, to which the third from the sun is home. On this scale, earth is just a particle of dust on a pebble in a sea of boulders. If this particle of dust was just a mile closer to the sun, we would be burned up and be unsustainable for life to exist. A mile further away and the temperatures would be so low, that the planet would be frozen solid in a permanent tundra winter. There would be no chance for life.

Even the planets were perfect, Jupiter being too large with too much gravity, Uranus being mostly methane gasses, and mercury being a smoldering hot liquid ball of metal. It seems that earth is a miracle planet, the perfect mixtures of minerals, water, oxygen, and the perfect placement. It seems we have won some type of universal lottery and it all landed smack dab in the middle of where we're supposed to be, in order for life to exist.

None of this is certain, however it's just the most adopted theory, excepted by the most educated people we have seen in our blip of existence, just theory. There are 92 naturally occurring elements, 115 if you want to count all, but some are man-made and some are theoretical, but scientists are "sure that they are there." Of the 92 naturally known elements, there are solids like iron, nickel, and gold, Liquids like water and oil, and gasses like hydrogen, nitrogen, and helium. On earth there is a perfect mixture of Stardust to make out our crust core and outer layer, mostly made of water which came from ice breaking off of passing comets. It then burned and melted as it hit our atmosphere. This happens so often that our planet is 70% water.

It kind of makes you feel good if you think about it, we are all here on this planet in the corner of this galaxy and a micro SPECT of the universe with just the great combination of elements in a perfect atmosphere.... prime real estate! When the earth was formed, it was a chaotic place. Full of raging volcanoes, intense dust storms, and unyielding oceans. The only place even remotely where life was sustainable, was where the land met the seas. In theory this is where life had begun.

(perhaps, that's why we feel so at home where the sea meets the land)

There are a lot of thoughts about how life happened. Science suggests that it was some type of primordial soup, bacteria from an asteroid, or in the water of a comet. But most agree that it came from water.

Religions have manuscripts and teachings dating back thousands of years, they say that all was a creation of a God or some form of deity who desired companionship or servitude. The theories, thoughts, and beliefs are endless. Some with very rational evidence and some not so much. There is however, a thought that I would like to touch on that does little to contradict both science and religion on the big question "why are we here?"

As if there actually had to be a real reason why we are here. Humans are just complicated creatures, pregnant with questions that just have to be delivered. There is a thought or theory that I have heard from both sides and mystics alike, that is able to tie into religion. The thought that everything you see, and everything you are, is just the universe experiencing itself. It sounds so mystical and scientific but leaves little room for religion to understand. This is not a theory on the soul or afterlife. Just one on the current life in the short time you're here to better understand, and think about why we are here.

So the universe explodes through the above said scenarios, statements, and theories, creating all we see, hear, smell, touch, taste, and think about. This happened through endless teachings, beliefs, and theories of how we got here through evolution, intelligent design, or just a plain happy accident on a perfectly scattered together rock revolving around a ball of fire flying through outer space. The fact of the matter is that, yes, we are here, nobody really knows why, and that to me is the beauty of it all. I might even say it's the point.

And with this thought, the universe, through some unexplainable way, had created itself and is now experiencing itself, leaving out the ability to be self-aware. I believe it's part of the beauty of the mystery of it all. Mystery is the universe's favorite flavor. It's a mystery how you got to be here today and a mystery where you will be tomorrow. It's a mystery why we are here, and a mystery who we are, or what we will become, or will become of us.

Mystery itself leads our life forms into one of the best, most creative aspects.... imagination. With imagination we have created all that we see. It was imagination that-spawned countries with imaginary lines to build walls. It was imagination that created all the technology, art, literature, and music.

Perhaps we are just the universe's imagination at play, dancing in the mystery of itself as it tries to become self-aware and at times it does through religious parables, scientific facts, and historical evidence that says we are just small glimpses into a mystery of the universe. It's so simple that our mousetrap minds would never fathom.

We are however here and now in a physical form, without a doubt children of the earth in the family tree of the universe. The stars were destroyed & the earth was created, and out of the earth came you. The same basic elements that make up earth, make up your body, and all is made from Stardust. Perhaps we are in the experience to note that we are made out of dirt and be humbled by that fact, but in our journey to realize that dirt we are made from comes from the stars.

What if the big bang theory was actually right and science was correct? What if God is real and religion was correct? Both can be right if the big bang theory was the cataclysm that caused "a"or "the" vibration. A vibration is just the waves of energy. Ebb and flow, up and down, waves of sound... Even light is just a vibration Interpreted by our brain.

There is a popular experiment that went viral on the Internet, where a person put sand over speakers playing certain frequencies of music. Different frequencies cause different patterns in the sand. When the experiment was done in the sand the patterns were brilliant.

According to certain religions that are very deep into meditation and Mantras, there is a vibration in the universe known as OM. When explained, the beginning of most mantras is OM, because it is the frequency at which the universe vibrates.

If frequencies can organize sand into brilliant patterns in seconds while on a speaker, what's to stop the thought that the Big Bang caused a sound echoing into the universe? And if that sound was the vibration of OM, and the vibration organized the chaos into the brilliance you see today?

If vibration is just waves caused by a cataclysm, and vibration is what organizes that cataclysm into patterns, then the universe is just a heartbeat of chaotic vibrations being organized by itself. The Big Bang causes galaxies....galaxies create stars....with stars solar systems are born, and that eventually become worlds like ours. Chaos into structure.

The same can be said about what happens in our small speck of dust that we call earth. Storms chaos create ripples that become waves, and these are waves that we ride in a dance of vibration replicating the chaos of creation.

The universe is the ocean

I am the ocean

You are the ocean

Our individuality

There's nothing more

Than a wave that is created

Travels across The ocean

And breaks up on a reef or beach

So to do we die

But nothing has changed

When the wave is gone

It hits the sand

And rolls back into the ocean

One day we too will break

But rejoice, for after we break

We will just recede ....

....back into the ocean.

CHAPTER 15

The first thing you feel, when you sell everything you own and walk away from all that you've built, is relief. Followed quickly, but a little bit lost. And then, perhaps a feeling of freedom that you never thought was possible. I could almost relate it to a zoo animal being released into the wild after years behind a cage. When that door opens and they run out into the prairie for the first time, I don't think they know what to do. I was no different. So I went for a surf.

I got a gym pass to shower, I was making money during the day and night by Ubering in all the cities that I traveled up and down the coast. I surfed whenever I wanted, and I had nobody to answer to. I had no rent or bills besides for my car. I did however have one attachment that had turned up out of nowhere. A beautiful girl named Taylor.

Her and I were very unofficial, but we were head over heels for each other in a different way. We would see each other as often as we could with our conflicting schedules (she had a job and I had a surf habit).

This is where I learned one of the best lessons of a freedom mindset. At first, when we started seeing each other, it was like heaven on earth. But soon became a living hell, just like any other relationship. It wasn't either of our faults. We were both just at different points of our journey.

She worked an insane amount of hours and came home to me, who had been surfing all day and had nothing to do. She would throw me a bunch of attitude out of nowhere and try and start a fight on a regular basis. I never understood it. Over time she became colder and colder towards me, and one day she was just so cold I didn't even know what to do with myself so I took off.

I drove down the street and at the end was a literal crossroads. I knew that if I turned right, I would go to Huntington Beach and Uber for the evening. I knew that if I turned left, I was heading north and I wasn't coming back. I turned left.

The only place that I felt comfortable and welcomed was a 15 Hour drive up the coast in Humboldt County. The irony was, when I was coming into San Francisco, I had received a phone call. A guy that I work for named Keith had just bought a farm and needed help. He asked me how fast I could get to Humboldt and I replied that I was halfway there.

I spent a few weeks up in Humboldt, working farms and seeing friends. I spent about a week up in Keith's farm and decided that I was going to be working for him pretty much full time. But first I had to go back to Huntington Beach, gather my things and say goodbye to Taylor.

After just a couple of weeks on the road, I could feel where I was being pulled in the flow. Southern California had lost its charm and northern California was now home. Everything in my life was pointing north.

I grabbed a couple of surfboards and a few things from a storage unit that I had, said my goodbyes to Taylor, and headed to Tahoe where I stayed a couple of weeks doing landscaping before eventually landing back in Humboldt.

The world was my oyster at this point and I could go in every direction I wanted. As I focused on the flow everything took me to Humboldt. And now that I'm here it is starting to make sense. The flow state was a very real thing and I was exactly where I was supposed to be and it was easy.

Within days I landed a spot for $300 a month that was pretty much overlooking the bay of Eureka. The backyard had a giant redwood forest behind the house. It was absolute heaven. I would often go check the surf at North jetty, but a lot of the time it was either 20 foot and maxing out or two-foot mush with seals in every direction.

There's a spot called camel rock that I started to grow fond of. It's a big long right hander that brakes behind a rock with a really good short break on the inside. Between this spot and the dunes, I was getting my fill of ocean time while hanging out with a bunch of humans in their flow state of life.

Looking back now, everything was perfect. I had friends that had a unique understanding, a beautiful place to live, and surf whenever I wanted. One of the best aspects was that Keith's wife had retired from United years earlier. She had passes for free flights and they had put me on their standby list. So basically I didn't have to pay for flights anymore which is one of the most expensive parts of traveling.

Another beautiful thing was that Keith had a house on the big Island of Hawaii. This just happened to be directly on the beach in Kona. Two beautiful surf spots right next to each other. One was called banyans and is where Shane Dorian actually grew up and learned to surf. The other is called Lymans, and as a goofy foot, might be my favorite left, besides Haggerty's in LA.

If I had not left the comfort of Huntington Beach, I would not have had these blessings. If I did not follow my flow in life just like I had learned on all those trim scenes from all of those hippies, I would not be full of health, free to travel across the world, and living in complete bliss. So there's something to be said about the flow state of life as well.

It was during this time that I got addicted to reading my favorite book that inspired this book. "West of Jesus" by Steven Kotler. He had done some serious research about flow states and the effects of adrenaline on the human brain. Mostly the effects of surfing on the human brain as well.

I was instantly addicted to this book. Not only had I learned about the stoke, the flow state, but now I'm learning about the effects of surfing on the brain which was actually why I started this journey to begin with. As it turns out I wasn't alone in my search or in my experiences.

In "west of Jesus" Steven travels the world in search of a myth known as "The conductor". It was definitely quite a narrative to follow while understanding flow states on the human mind. My journey had started off wondering why I was so different, and now has turned into chasing the flow of waves and the flow in life. I recommend this book if you are ever chasing flow as well.

I spent the next year and a half literally going everywhere I was pulled. There was no obstacle in my way as long as I was going where I was supposed to be. I spent half the year in Hawaii at Keith's house, and the other half up and down the coast surfing and music festival hopping. It was absolute bliss.

The hardest part of the journey was going back home. Whether it be to Huntington Beach, or Arizona where my parents live. Every time I went home for Christmas to Arizona, it felt like I got stuck back in the maze for a second. During the holidays I would drink myself stupid. When I would go home I was always a little bit sick, lost, and very out of my flow.

The only thing my dad ever really talked about was football, work, and Jesus. Three things I grew up talking about, none of which I talked about anymore. It definitely felt like it stagnated my life to even join the conversation. There's nothing wrong with those three things, but that's not what kept me going ...except for... in my adult life when I went back and studied the New Testament and the path Jesus took.

As it turns out, Jesus walked on water so to me he was a surfer. But there was more to the story that met the eye. I had read the Bible growing up because I was forced into it. Most of what Jesus's philosophy was, was literally giving up everything and following God. Is that what I was doing? It's definitely no wonder that I was establishing surfing as my religion.

"It is easier for the camel to fit through the eye of a needle, then it is for a rich man to get into the kingdom of God" this is the passage that stuck out to me most when I reread the New Testament. As it turns out, rich people, when they get money seem to get really hesitant about anything they do in life. Even 2000 years ago Jesus was telling a rich man to give everything away and go for a walk with God.(flow)

The funny part was, he did it around 30 years old. The exact same age that I was when I sold everything in Huntington Beach and began my journey. I'm definitely not Jesus, I was just making the connection that it seemed like he maybe, left his job as a carpenter, and began his journey around the same age.

Jesus preached about peace & love and wandered around homeless, hanging out with a bunch of sinners. He was judged every step of his way. But what he found was "The kingdom of God" but what he found was possibly the same thing that Buddha had found years before on his journey.

The Man we all know as Buddha, was put in a castle and lived a privileged life. His father wanted to hide him from pain or suffering that life endures. One day, he snuck out of the lush life that he had been living. He went around the town he lived in, and saw for the first time people that were sick and dying, people that were poor and old, and people that were dead. He did not know how to react except to go on his own journey.

Around the age of 35, Siddhartha found enlightenment under a tree. He too preached peace and love, Detachment, and meditation. The reason that I bring this up is that while I was traveling, I had to be completely detached from what I was doing in order for the flow state to happen. I noticed that the more detached I was, the more the flow state seemed prevalent. It was like the less I cared, the more I was in the zone. The less I wanted things, the more I seemed to obtain everything I desired.

While surfing, or any other sport for that matter, getting in the zone is something that all athletes talk about. The best Surfer seems to be the one that looks like he's doing the most effortless surfing in the most critical parts of a wave. Perhaps the most enlightened person is somebody who lives in a flow state of life by barely trying and completely wanting nothing.

I was definitely in a flow state, and in my flow in life. I had no possessions, I had no direction and I had never been happier.

CHAPTER 16

I would have to say that the best lessons I've ever had in my entire life have been about humility. Whether I was talking too much Just before having my ass handed to me by a guy half my size. Or if I was getting cocky in Hawaii after getting barreled on a 10-foot wave, thinking about how I was on top of the world, only to be pummeled by a 15 foot wave that was just behind it. We have all had those days, especially during the winter, where you try to scratch into a wave that just barely passes you by, only to turn around and see the mother of all ass kickers about to mow you down.

I would say that the best fighters weren't talking trash outside the ring. A lot of the time you could look at a Mike Tyson fight, and for most of his career the opponents would just sit and talk, only to be knocked out in the ring. And I am sure we have all had that experience with meeting a guy at a party who looked the look, he talked the talk, and the second you got them out and anything over 6 foot, he looked like a wet cat in the water.

Surfing is a bit like what you would see in a kung fu movie. The second a Bruce Lee movie ends, everybody in the room turns into ninjas. I have watched people live their entire life through kung fu movies, and they truly thought that they were something until they were put into a position where they had to be that guy. I once knew a guy who claimed to be a Master of karate, I mean he walked the walk, and he talked the talk. But I started noticing after spending a lot of time with him, that any time there was confrontation he was the first to hightail it out of the room.

Surfing is without a doubt one of the most popular sports on the planet. Hollywood has made it seem like you can move to Hawaii from Arizona and learn to big waves like Rick Kane in one winter. But anybody knows that it takes the average Surfer a minimum of about four years to really learn how to surf. That's four years of getting your ass handed to you by the ocean. That's four years of being consistent in the water at least three times a week, and the water in January when it's freezing, in the water despite temperature, shark sightings, jellyfish warnings, and watching everybody do the stingray shuffle on the beach. Surfing everything from 6 to 8 foot closeouts, to 2 foot groveling waves on an on shore windy day. The commitment Has to be real or you're a straight up kook!

It is for this reason that we celebrate people that rip. It's not just because their style is good and the babes are watching from shore. It's a respect thing, it's respect for their commitment to mastering the sport. That means that they have been beating on their craft religiously and now you see where that work has come to fruition in just a six second wave.

It never gets old when you meet somebody who is landlocked in Arizona or somewhere so far from the ocean you know they could never actually be a ripper, and they sit and talk to you with the lingo and jargon that they hear in the movies. As Turtle said in the north shore, "You can usually tell the guys lame by the way they wear their shorts". For me, I can usually tell how long someone has been surfing or out of the water by the way he paddles.

With every other sport on the planet you already start by doing that sport. Something like snowboarding for example, since people always want to compare it to surfing (A sport in which is not comparable to anything else.) in snowboarding, you already begin by standing on the board. All you have to do is learn how to turn and stop, and then you get to the advanced tricks.

When you begin surfing you have to learn about the ocean first. Riptides, currents, undertows, hazards in the water, and a galaxy of other useful information before you even begin to paddle. And paddling just happens to be one of the most difficult aspects of surfing to master.

Then, you have to learn how to duck dive, fall properly, know which wave is rideable and where to start paddling into it, how to drop in and read the wave, and then you begin surfing. Not to mention every other sport on the planet starts with a solitary surface that you can just do the same thing over and over again and master. In the ocean you have to wait an insane amount of times in between the set waves.

One of the most frustrating aspects of surfing that a lot of people don't talk about, especially in Hollywood, is how long it takes to get a wave in between sets. I have gone out surfing on plenty of days where I was completely skunked. After years of surfing, putting my time in, surfing 2 foot to 10 foot, taking my licks, surfing the most crowded lineups I've ever seen in Southern California, and still I went home without a wave after a three-hour session. Talk about humility.

Some of the most interesting people I have ever met in my entire life, have come from a background that was less than nurturing. People that I find interesting or people that overcome obstacles such as being born in poverty, having their parents split up or die at a young age, living with drug abuse or alcohol abuse, living in a place where you had to fight for your meals or even scavenge for them.

If a person can make it through all of that, and still come out the other side with a decent mind, it's usually a miracle but when it happens it's quite a sight to see, and a person to know. I've known people whose parents were drug addicts, lived on the streets, had abusive family members, and against all odds became a really decent human being, and those are the people that I am inspired by the most.

In surfing, no matter what you do unless you are extraordinarily selective and extremely lucky, if you put your time in and play with the fire of the sport, you will get burnt. Not just burnt by other surfers, but you will be burnt by the universe and the ocean alike. There will be days when the waves are perfect, but none of them will come to you. You watch guys get barreled out of their minds and come out only to be taking table scraps the entire session and heading back to your car with a sour face.

This is the disciplinary aspect of humility. It's like gold that you can grab with your hands but it melts through your fingers. Like a day where you are lined up for the perfect wave.

CHAPTER 17

What is it that drives somebody to get up at 5 AM to catch the morning glass? There is a spiritual sense to it that keeps us motivated to tap in to the source. There is also an undeniable drive to be able to ride any board, any wave, in any condition. But there is also a communal sense to it as well. Just to be part of a Global tribe all across the planet of people that you have something in common with.

"I just surf because it's fun to go out and ride with your friends" - Matt Johnson

Big Wednesday.

The statement holds true for every Surfer and their heart. The people I grew up with surfing the short breaks and the big days have a bond with me unlike any other. Every surfer has that group that even if they're not in the same circles in life they always get together in the morning to catch the waves before the wind hits.

For me I had a crew, and this crew was full of unique individuals with different personalities that all came out in their surfing and their life. I was a bit of a lazy surfer. I like to get up at about 8 o'clock and mosey onto the beach while sipping on a coffee and having a bagel, only to crawl into my wetsuit and grab some waves. But as I started making Surfer friends I had people crawling through my window at 4 AM to wake me up. Growing up, my good friend Curtis, growing up, used to crawl through my window with a cup of coffee and wake me up no matter what the waves were doing. He was perpetually stoked.

My friend Kyle and I would do the same, whoever was first to wake up, would drag each other down at the beach no matter how big or small the waves were. Between Curtis and Kyle, I would say that my surfing abilities had doubled because I trusted them in the water. If I were to get knocked out by my board or have a really bad wipeout, they were always watching. They knew I was watching them as well.

Sometimes, just for the comedy sake of it, we would cheer each other into the waves that were completely unmakeable and if you didn't go the hazing was real.

I once watched a documentary on how to live to be over 100 years old. All of the people that lived well into their golden years had certain things in common with each other. They all danced, traveled often, garden, strangely enough they drank alcohol every day (not a lot of alcohol just some) and the most important factor was to have some type of fellowship.

A lot of people who are religious live a long and happy life. I believe that it's because they all gather a couple times a week with people that are like-minded. The people that I know that are depressed in life usually isolate themselves whether it be purposely or just because they don't have any real friends. The one thing the surfing community has brought me, was the closest people with a very special connection.

In brain chemistry, you have the reward systems that I already covered in the earlier half of the book. The reward system that I'm talking about at the moment is oxytocin. The fact that you can show up, even if you're just a weekend warrior and surf some crumbly waves with your friends on a Saturday and Sunday does a lot to your brain and your well-being. Oxytocin is the chemistry of fellowship or family. That's what you feel when you relate.

To get up stoked every morning and then go see people that you can relate with, brings a type of closure to your day. It's like having a family. The people that I learned to surf with were all much older than me when I was a kid. I started surfing at 15 and this guy that lived in my neighborhood saw me walking to the bus stop every weekend with my board. One day he took a friend and I to the beach. It was like a mentor but more like an older brother. His name was Kelly, not to be mistaken with Kelly Slater, but he was without a doubt a phenomenal Surfer.

Super old-school style with a 10-foot board. He was up at 4 AM every single day hitting the waves. Whether they were 2 feet or 10 feet with no leash, and riding slow easy lines. He tried 100 times to convert me to a longboard which never really took until I was much older. He was without a doubt one of the most important people in my life.

From the moment I became a surfer, when somebody else claimed to be a surfer, it would change my view of them. It was almost like speaking another language, and you found others that spoke that language.

When I traveled through Central America by myself, I went to all surf destinations. While traveling, I found other people who were traveling by themselves and just chasing waves like I was. It was like an instant brotherhood (or sisterhood) and we usually linked up for a couple surf trips. Sometimes you find some local guy or a pro that knows about some secret spots. You guys would go adventuring through the chaos that is a third world country, only to ride a few waves and have a beer afterwards. Like meeting a long lost family.

I've also traveled to non-surf destinations and it doesn't seem to have the same type of magic. Usually while I'm traveling, I'm chasing waves, the party, or the women. And on a good surf trip I usually find all three. It was kind of what drove me to the edges of the map through Mexico, Hawaii and Central America.

But after a good solo trip, you usually end up with another 20 or 30 new friends. I always end up traveling to other destinations where they're from. You go visit and they let you crash and surf at their local break. It's very rare that I found a family like that in any other form or activity. I did spend some years traveling up and down the coast eating psychedelics and festival hopping. I can say that I found a relatively close connection in the music and hippie communities, but not nearly the same.

There's just something about surfing. There's just something about meeting others who have done the work in the water and developed the discipline, especially those that put the time in. I respect a good Surfer because I know that they had to start at the beginning. They had to use their artistic genius nature to be able to understand how to carve a wave properly.

When you can find somebody who has put just as much time in as you, it's almost like two kung fu masters have met, and then you test each other in the water. A lot of times when somebody says they can surf, you start sizing them up with the language they use and then the next step is to meet them in the water. They look the look, they talk the talk, but when it's time to walk they wobble.

I've always said that the only thing that I'm cocky about in life is surfing and that's because I mastered it. I beat on that craft on a daily basis and took my licks. I took every clean upset in ice cold frigid waters, my back had been sunburnt to blisters, been stung by jellyfish, seen sharks, stepped on stingrays, choked on water, and pulled people out of the water like the kids that scratched me up trying to save them as they're freaking out, to the bodies that I pulled out of the water that were less fortunate. I've seen people break their neck, hit their board, knock all their teeth out, slam into the pier, and watched a few people lose their lives in the pursuit of waves.

This all created a level of respect when you meet somebody who has spent their time in the water. The more time you put in the water, the more you'll see things and understand situations, and the more your fellow surfer will respect what you've gone through and the discipline that you've developed.

But it's not all dreary, most of the days you go out and you get 3 to 4 foot waves with some of your best friends and strangers. Everyone is in the same pursuit as you. As the studies have shown it takes fellowship to complete happiness. So the fellowship that you develop is one that is important, not only to your psyche but to your length of life and your everyday happiness.

So what drives us to the ocean? It could be the pursuit of happiness, it could be a longer life, it could be an adventure. Whatever it is, it's always personal to each individual, but it's always the same proving ground for the same tribe that's all over the world.

I as of now and my best memories have been in the ocean. I've never laughed so hard or been so frustrated in one place. It's kind of like falling in love, it is this beautiful mystical magical thing that happens to you. But just like a lover it could quickly go from heaven to hell in a matter of seconds. You could be paddling for your dream wave and miss it just in time to turn around to live a nightmare. There have been people that got caught up in the food chain of the event and lost their lives to oceanic monsters, and people they got rides in their life that made them cry.

Laird Hamilton got one of the biggest waves ever surfed in Tahiti, at the time, it was like winning the World Series as he described it. He sat in the channel that day and wept. He cried like somebody who I just knocked the ball out of the park when the bases were loaded and they were down by three. I too have had waves that had me really check myself in life.

You go home and you just keep visualizing that one wave that made your session. You fall asleep seeing it & you wake up seeing it, you see it for the rest of your life, and just like a drug addict you chase that same feeling all around the world for the rest of your surfing life.

And if you were to catch that winning wave during your session, the only thing that makes it way better, is if you have your crew of friends that see it happen. I for one can say that I've seen my friends get probably the best waves of their life, and the best wave I have ever gotten I came spitting out of a tube and almost ran over my friend that was screaming at the top of his lungs. It makes it that much better because after all , all surfers are giant show offs.

When you get to the level where you can actually surf, it's all about using that board as a paintbrush and the wave as your canvas. If you could groove with good style, and grease it all the way through, and have your friend see while you're doing it, that's the respect, that's the fellowship, that's the ultimate ride. To ride well with nature with your personal friendships that you develop in this blip of existence that we call life.

CHAPTER 18

I was living my best life, full of freedom, and I had nobody to answer to. Money was something I didn't even think about most of the time. As long as my life was flowing, it seemed like the money was flowing like a river as well. It was never more than I needed, in fact it was always exactly what I needed and nothing less.

But just like anything else in life, there's always a balance. Right at the peak of my bliss, I found out my father was sick. Colon cancer. I was told that they were very optimistic about him beating it.

After an unsuccessful operation, I went and sat with him for five months while he did chemo in Arizona. I was losing my mind the entire time being that far away from the ocean. But sometimes you have to focus on what's important. After a few months I decided that I needed to go get some waves.

I caught a bus to California and got some waves just before hopping a plane to Hawaii. In Hawaii I was so depressed about my father's sickness that it was difficult to surf. It was definitely an interesting experience. More than anything I just drank myself stupid the entire time I was there. After about three months in Hawaii, I went back to Northern California to pack and head to Peru.

There was something that was always calling me to Peru for a couple reasons, I've always wanted to do an Ayahuasca ceremony. Not to mention, Peru is known as the land of the endless lefts. As a goofy footed surfer, that was quite appealing to me.

I had tried to go to Peru three times before that, and something always happens. This time was no different, my passport was going to expire in five months and it has to be valid for six months to get in the country. As disappointed as I was, I realized that the most important place I should probably be was next to my father in Arizona. It wasn't like surfing was fun at this point anyway.

I went to Arizona and sat next to his bed for about another month before I had to leave, get a break from the depression, and get more waves. At this point I noticed that my surf sessions we're starting to span out. Five times a month and then four times a month, they just kept spreading out until I didn't surf for a whole month.

I went back to California for one of my last surf sessions for a very long time, I didn't know it at the time but I was about to be landlocked. While I was in California, I was doing some work putting up Christmas lights, when I got a call.

My father was given three months to live. You're not really trained to understand a phone call like that. But I knew what I was going to have to do. I told him I was on my way, and he told me to finish up work because he was going to drive to Florida as his last hurrah.

When I was done in Orange County, I got a call from him. As it turns out, he got entirely too sick to drive back home from Florida. I ended up flying out and driving him home. He said he was more than capable of taking care of himself even though we all begged to differ.

There was a swell hitting California's coast in January plus I was going to do some music in a studio with a good friend in Huntington Beach. I flew out for the End of January swell and was having the time of my life. And while understanding the balance of things I got another phone call. My father really needed somebody to take care of him.

February 14 I got a call that he had fallen and was not able to take care of himself. I volunteered to be the one to take care of him for the rest of his life. This means going to landlocked Arizona where there are no waves. This meant taking care of a sick person that was not going to get any better...and no waves for the foreseeable future. But when tragedy strikes, you have to be there especially if it's somebody close to you, and it's their last days.

My father and I were not the best of friends in life, but we were nowhere near enemies. We just saw life differently. He worked from 4 AM to 9 PM and only took time off for football and church. A very simple person to me. In his early years, he was a big-time drug dealer that was busted and found Jesus in jail.

When he got out of jail, he rounded my brother and I up and moved us to Arizona when we were kids. He did this so he could get away from Long Beach, which is where all the trouble was caused. He never really started going to church even though he found Jesus, until after he was growing weed in the mountains around where we lived and the rangers had busted him.

To his credit he actually got away. I must've been about 10 yea   when he came in looking like a mountain man with a giant beard and long hair.   oke us up and said that we were going to California. Little did I know the cops were looking for him. On this particular trip to California, he cut his hair and shaved his beard. As soon as we got back to Arizona we were at church every Sunday.

He eventually told the story to the whole church years later. I was pretty tripped out about the actual events that took place and how I remembered them. He said he was running from helicopters and rangers as he hid in a bush. He was quite the storyteller and in the version he told me, he could see his face in the cops boots as they walked by the bushes he was hiding in.

While hunkered down praying that he was going to get away, he said that he made a deal with God. The deal was he would clean up his life and go to church for the rest of it while doing nothing else drug related, if he could just get him out of that situation. After running all night from the rangers and helicopters, he jumped in a river at the bottom of the mountain and swam to civilization.

I have to admit, most of his stories were pretty gnarly. When I go to Long Beach, if I meet an old school person that's been there their whole life, and they find out that I am my father's son, it's nothing but respect after that. I'm sure there's a lot that I will never understand or know. A lot of his friends talk about his gangster years, but I only knew him as a workaholic Christian.

In November 2018 they gave him three months to live. I sat with him from February 14 until September 9, 2019, the day he passed. There was nothing easy about sitting next to a cancer patient. I have done it multiple times in my life before, but this was definitely the most intimate.

I have no regrets about sitting with him in his last days. I aged about 10 years, my health declined and I fell off the wagon and into a world of drinking myself into the darkness. It started the second he didn't have a pulse. As soon as he died, it was like all the stress that I had been enduring head popped like a cork.

I was so out of my mind, that I was yelling at his dead body as we waited for the corner, I attacked my brother, I cursed the world. I have no regrets about any of this because it was a huge learning experience and I had made my apologies.

When it comes to a flow state, it was nowhere to be found when I was sitting stagnant and not moving around. I did what I had to do and the job was now done. One thing was definitely certain. After sitting around for nine months of pure stress in a landlocked house, I needed to grieve for a while, and for that I knew that I needed to get some waves.

While being landlocked in Arizona, I did have a lot of time to think, journal, and research on the ultimate flow state of surfing and life. My search for the secrets of the universe. I had a lot of time to read and ponder while I was Performing hospice. While I was in a place of my life that was nowhere near a flow state, there were some epiphanies to be had.

Sometimes it seems like when the thing you want most is taken away, and distanced out of reach, it becomes clearer how to obtain and explain it.

CHAPTER 19

The insight of surfing is definitely one that runs deep. Whether it be the history of the sport, being the only recreational sport recorded 3000 years ago. Also its royal background and hierarchy of the lineup. And, its modern day fame where we have some of the highest paid athletes on the planet, it's one of the most watched sports, being viewed by every continent and one of the only sports besides soccer to do so.

To even call surfing a sport to me is a bit facetious. I know people that have dedicated their entire life to chasing waves. In fact, I know people in droves that Have done it. I don't know too many people who would sell everything they own and go live on a golf course. But I can count off the top of my head at least 5 that I know personally that have sold everything and live on a beach somewhere just surfing waves.

People might vacation to Hawaii for the golf and to relax, I vacation to Hawaii and sleep in the jungle to ride waves all winter long. When waves are all you need, it's a confusing feeling to watch the rest of the world do what it does. What do you do when you have everything you need and it doesn't make sense to anybody else?

I was never a very good student in school or the best at working a corporate job, because all I could think about are waves. But when I entered the lineup at my local break, that's when I felt good about myself. No audience in the stands, no scoreboard, no paycheck or bank account, it's not what you drive, or how big your house is, it's all about riding the wave, riding it well, and doing it with style.

Living life one wave at a time instead of paycheck to paycheck is quite a scary leap of faith. But it's one that I encourage every person to try at least once., especially if they're not happy with your current situation. There was a time when I was not happy with my current situation. I took the leap of faith and grew my wings on the way down.

Like I had explained, I was truck driving 70 hour weeks when I was 26 and only thinking about waves. I then quit my job and flew to Costa Rica by myself without telling anybody where I was going. It was the trip of a lifetime as if the universe favors the brave. Upon my return I realized that it was something else to this life that surfing has taught me. It was a type of flow state. One that I can't really explain to you in words, you have to feel it.

You have to go to the edge of the map and feed your reward systems. You have to face your fears and learn to have faith. I'm not asking you to become a homeless person, begging for change. The people you see doing that usually have some type of mental, drug or alcohol problem. I am living proof that when you check out of society and follow your bliss, the universe decides right then and there to start rewarding you.

Most people travel to far off destinations to enjoy the comforts that they have at home. They go to Hawaii to stay in a room that looks like the room in their house, they sit and watch

TV and go on a tour. But for surfers, the excitement for travel is chasing waves to far off destinations in remote locations. We seek a reef break or a point break that was discovered by a pioneer of surfing a long time ago. We rarely have commodities or roads for that matter, to get where we need to go. We dive off into unknown waters, with unknown dangers all for the thrill of the ride.

We pay top dollar to fly to dangerous places, to live like homeless people in order to chase that high that we get from the perfect ride. Might be sounding a little cliché right now but that's because words can't explain it. The more I try to explain to people I meet on airplanes, on the bus, or family, the more I sound like some type of brain-fried hippie who just enjoys the freedom of not having a job. The saying goes that "only a surfer knows the feeling". And that's because it can't be expressed in words, as Andy Irons was quoted saying "It's like being kissed by God."

There has to be something to it if the tribe of surfers all around the world are constantly dealing with sunburn backs, bouncing off the reef, frigid waters, sharks, sand rash, polluted water, skin cancer, third World dangers, and empty wallets. Through all of this, the reward systems are high, and the flow state is met. It's a place that very few will ever find in this life, a place where you lose your mind but you find your soul.

As the band Wookiefoot wrote in one of my favorite songs "You will never see a hearse with the trailer hitch." "There will be no pockets in the pants you're buried in." In a consumer market, people are concerned with piling money and possessions. It seems the goal is to die with the most stuff and make as many people sad at your funeral as possible. But rich or poor all humans end up in the same grave. And the only thing that you can truly take with you to the other side, if there is one, is your experience.

One of my favorite quotes is "We are not humans having a spiritual experience, we are spirits having human one." This gives me great comfort in the life choices that I've made. Like giving up all my possessions and truly living my path, I've witnessed my magic that I cannot even explain. I would say that surfing is the foundation for every choice I've ever made, and in that regard to this day, I still have no regrets. I've never regretted quitting my job, surfing more on zero dollars a day and journeying outside of my comfort zone. This choice was based on the fact that I surf.

I know that every single human has within them the desire to be free and live life on their own terms. That is after all, why people want lots of money. Some of it is so they can buy whatever they want, but mostly I believe the people just want to live a life where nobody can tell them what to do. A life where they can go wherever they want. Everybody just wants their own slice of the pie and doesn't want anybody to tell them how it tastes.

Surfing can give you this type of freedom without you even knowing it. After all, when you're out there, it's just you and the ocean. Pirates and sailors alike have always talked about the freedom that the ocean brings you. People travel for thousands of miles from inland destinations just to stare at the ocean.

But whether you are a corporate conglomerate who spends the weekend in Malibu on his longboard with 500 other people out at the point, to enjoy the ocean and a wave or two, or if you are a full-time traveling gypsy like myself, in search of the perfect ride, the ride where time slows down and nothing else seems to exist. We are part of the same tribe of people, all around the world. Through my research of why I love surfing, my experiences of understanding that I do, and traveling the planet while meeting others who feel the same way I do about the ocean, the ride, and the experience, I can truly say that I have no regrets about my life decisions to dedicate my life to the ocean. At least in this time of existence...... I am living, and in love with life.

CHAPTER 20

While sitting in Arizona, I had a lot of time to reflect. My father was extremely religious and had much of his church coming in and out of the house. They did a lot of praying, a lot of preaching to me as well. The pastor even came over with a picture of him and I when he first baptized me. To be baptized in the Christian religion is to be hand-in-hand with their Messiah. It is to be "saved"

Little did most of them know that I had a different religion now. I had danced with God on the ocean and a flow state that I never got while singing in church on a Sunday morning. But the idea of a baptism in water being So significant to the Christian religion had me pondering.

A baptism is described as being fully or partially submerged in water in a right of passage. And in some religions the baptism is one of the most important steps of being initiated into said religion. After a baptism, the person is now responsible for their own sins.

Most warriors would never have been considered a warrior unless they had been in a war. Once in a war and survived, it is said that you were baptized in the crucible of war. Also in prison terms, if somebody baptized you, it means that they kicked your ass. Whether it's being submerged in water, or getting your ass kicked, or even just some type of rights of passage, every true religion has some type of baptism.

When I had first begun surfing, the older gentleman that I surfed with would Haze me to my wits end. We would show up at the beach at 4 AM before the sun came up and the fog was still thick. All the old men still sipping their coffee next to the near dead fires on the beach would send me out into the ocean by myself no matter how big the waves were or how visible the environment was.

Some mornings the fog would be so thick you could not see the water. "Hey Blake, go check the waves and tell me how they are." "You gotta earn it grom!!!" They used to shout at me as I would paddle out by myself completely full of fear. In those days I still worried about sharks (not that I ever stopped) I would worry about drowning, or hitting my board, or even just having to take 6 to 8 foot waves on the head for 20 minutes at a time.

Little did I know that these mentors of mine were actually making me a much better surfer. I had to face the same fears that they had to go through when they were younger. After a few years of what I thought was punishment, I had begun to get up early and go by myself. I'd hop the fence before the beach was opened and the waves got crowded with close to no fear. I would get waves to myself all morning and when people began arriving, I would be all surfed out because I got every wave I wanted.

Now that I'm older, I definitely saw this as some type of rights of passage, and something that I would definitely pass on to anyone under my wing. There's something to be said for doing something challenging and tough that forces you to put yourself out there and face your fear.

Most of those days I would get the longest hold downs I would ever encounter and I would be doing it alone. That's where you really learned to stay focused and calm. That's where you really learn what you're made of.

Most rites of passage usually have one thing in common, you have to do it by yourself. Nobody else is going to paddle out for you, nobody else is going to pull you out of a really bad wipeout, and no one else is going to save your ass when you're caught inside. It's just you and the ocean at that point, you're in God's playground.

It happens to anyone who's ever been caught inside on a really big day, that is, every true surfer that decides to paddle out in anything over 6 feet. I think I can view that punishment, when you're actually caught inside trying to hold onto your board for dear life as a type of baptism. It's definitely some type of rights of passage when you take 20 waves on the head and you feel like you're wrestling an alligator just to keep your board in your hands, to be able to keep paddling and make it to the lineup, is a feat in itself.

If we are talking in prison terms, like getting your ass kicked, then being caught inside is that rite of passage that is your baptism. Of course, I would see it more of a rite of passage and a challenge. It definitely resembles a baptism, covered in water. Taking a 10 foot wave on the head that detonates right in front of you, for anyone who has ever experienced it, knows that it is not the most pleasing feeling you've ever had. It's extraordinarily violent, your legs are by your ears and you don't know which way is up. If your board gets pulled out of your arms you just pray that your leash doesn't break. If god forbid that broke, you're in for quite a challenge in the form of swimming against the current's to try and make it back to the beach.

Native American culture has something called a Sundance. This is where when a boy becomes a man, he gets tied up to a post and tortured without food or water for up to three days. If he survives, he is a man. They see it as an extreme form of rites of passage. I wouldn't exactly call that a baptism. But the rights of passage no doubt. I believe every time you get caught inside on a hair-raising day, this is the surfers equivalent to this style rites of passage. Although it's nowhere near as painful as a Sundance, it's definitely more consistent. As a Sundance is only done once in a lifetime, you never know when you're going to get caught inside, and it can happen daily.

In truth, I would say that the ultimate baptism for a surfer is to get barreled and come out. As Bruce Brown said in the Endless Summer "In surfing, the ultimate thing is to get barreled." I wouldn't even say that it's the hardest thing to do in surfing, but it is without a doubt the hardest thing to find, to read, and it takes nerves of steel mixed with the right conditions and years of dedication to get deep inside of one and come out.

I had begun surfing around 15 years old and dedicated almost every day to it from then until now. I have stated and it has been said multiple times, it takes a surfer years to really learn how to surf. I can admit that in my surfing career, the first few years I claimed a lot of barrels. It wasn't that I thought I was lying, it's that I really thought I was getting barreled. Maybe some deep pockets or a couple crumbles on the head and I would throw up the claim as if I was in a pro surfing video. But only after years of dedication, did I actually pull into something that would be considered a barrel for the very first time.

It was about 6 AM at Anderson Street in Sunset Beach, when it happened for the first time. I was about three years into surfing. Kelly and I paddled out after hearing that there were some pretty good sandbars forming after a large swell. I remember rolling up to the spot, checking the surf and seeing the waves go top to bottom in a very square shape. It wasn't that big, maybe 3 to 4 feet, but the waves were crashing and making sounds like thunder.

I remember being able to walk out to the lineup because the sandbars were so shallow at the time, and the tide was at a negative low. I was tripping out about how good of shape it was and yet the waves were detonating on a sandbar that was about 2 feet deep. I was a decent surfer at this point and was able to paddle into almost anything, but this particular day I wasn't ready for the steepness of the wave and got pitched at least five times before I finally caught anything. The first one I made the drop on, turned out to be "The wave."

I remember making the drop, and setting my line while watching the entire thing begin to break in front of me. It wasn't that big, maybe about 4 feet or so, but completely square. At this point it was either ditch and jump in the water or pull in and hang on.

There's something that happens to all surfers at certain points of their careers. Something almost mystical. It can usually take some magic board on a magic wave to come together with all of the elements. It usually takes your mind to not only focus, but to not focus at the same time. It takes going into what they call a flow state.

The samurai of Japan were experts in sword fighting. They have thousands of scrolls recorded over hundreds of years that teach the secrets of this combat style. One of the most important things that they record is "getting out of the mind". According to the samurai, If you are too much in your mind while in combat, you will not make the correct moves. You must find your flow state in order to survive in battle.

Every Surfer you talk to has had waves where it felt like somebody else was doing the surfing. Where they made the perfect drop with ease, only to set their line and shred the entire thing like a professional. It almost feels like you get possessed for a second, or even that you're watching yourself do it from out of your body. This was one of those moments.

I felt like an alien had taken over my body that knew exactly what to do in that split second decision of pulling into the barrel. I wanted to straighten off and ditch, but my feet had other plans. I tucked perfectly under the lip without it hitting me, pulled in and put my arm in the wave like I've seen a thousand times in videos of my favorite surfers. It was hard to explain the fact that I felt like I was watching myself from different angles... outside of my body.

At this point, time completely stopped. It almost felt like it wasn't me. I had a focus that I've only seen in a hunter's face. It felt like molecules of water were slowly going by me at 1000 frames per second and I could not only see them clear and slow but I could look at them and refocus. And just as slow and as possessed as it felt, I then felt time start to speed up as I was shot out the barrel with perfect form. A moment I will never forget. An outer body experience? An inner body experience? I couldn't even explain it. I paddled out back to Kelly and when he looked at me, I had nothing to explain. He could see it on my face. I just got barreled for the very first time.

I felt like doing a dance on the beach, I felt like praising the heavens, I felt like I had just had my first religious experience where I didn't have to fake it and it wasn't just something that I was trying to believe. It was something that I actually lived, and an experience that was mine and mine alone. It was my own religious experience. My own baptism.

I wanted to tell the world, I wanted to spread the word. I wanted to explain what it felt like, but there were no words. I ran home and told my grandma, I ran home and called my girlfriend. I told all the dudes at school. Nobody seemed to think it was a very big deal. But it was a big deal. What I had experienced was more than just a guy with foam and fiberglass and a rubber suit sliding across some type of water. What I had experienced felt esoteric.

I grew up religious, I was baptized by a pastor, I sang the songs at church, I had put my hands in the sky for Jesus, I had even cried during prayer before because I felt the joy of the Holy Spirit. But nothing came close to this. It was like an acid trip without taking acid, it was like an orgasm without having sex, it was better than both put together, it was better then all three combined.

The problem with it was that it happened so fast it's really hard to remember, it's really hard to explain, but I had been bitten. I was bitten by something and I was now addicted to something that I would chase my entire life. The eye of the storm of that barrel was my own personal dragon to chase. I knew that there was never going to be another peek of life that would even compare in this plane of existence. And I knew right then and there, that is what I was going to live for, maybe even die for.

It is a very difficult thing to explain things that cannot be explained. The only equivalent that I could ever compare it to was maybe a DMT trip, which I have done many times, but even those still don't hold a candle to the psychedelic effects of getting all of the elements together around the world to meet you in the perfect spot to have an unexplainable experience.

CHAPTER 21

Accidental enlightenment

What is the goal or achievement that any human is chasing in anything that they do? Everybody has a different goal and agenda for why it is that we do the crazy things we do on this planet. For some people it's riches, for some people it's an adrenaline rush, for some people it's peace. Whatever it is, there's something that's driving us all towards that goal.

I think some people think that chasing money will bring them a type of piece that they are looking for, and perhaps chasing it is just the rush they need. I always called it chasing the reward system. The reward systems that I talked about that are in your head like dopamine, serotonin, and oxytocin. They say money can't buy happiness but scientists discovered that it can, but only at $70,000 a year. Anymore and any less you're miserable.

Everything in moderation... ...including moderation.

So if the goal is not to make billions of dollars in order to be happy, then what is the true key to happiness? Perhaps it's the life of moderation given the fact that $70,000 is the golden number that would keep you in your pursuit of happiness. Some people find it in meditation, some people find it in drugs, and some find it and just have family. Meditation dopamine, drug serotonin, family oxytocin. These are the chemicals that get released and they make us happiest.

So tapping into those chemicals, and into your happiness perception of life is what we're chasing? There are people that say they find it with an hour of yoga a day. That would be the endorphins. But is it really something physical we're chasing if our physical form is just that of the finite?

Could it be something spiritual? Something more along the lines of what the Buddhists have been trying to achieve high up in the mountains away from civilization in search of enlightenment. Enlightenment itself is a loaded word especially these days in a time of snake oil salesman, absolute preposterous hoaxes, and in a time of pure fake news, scientific evidence, and false claims.

What if enlightenment was just a combination of giving your body everything that is needed in order to feed your spirit? What if Heaven was actually here on earth? And even deeper, what if it was actually in our minds? These questions have plagued me enough to have pondered what Enlightenment truly is.

If you ask a common person, they'll tell you that Enlightenment is becoming one with the universe. If you ask a monk, he might say the same thing, but that's in itself a loaded answer...loaded with literally everything. One might be able to experience being one with everything, but how is it articulated to the rest of us who are still wandering in purgatory lost?

My answer lay within the confines of this book as a whole. Everything from feeding our reward systems, to getting all the sunlight one could ever need, grounding yourself out, everything science can measure, and everything your soul feels is right in front of every surfer while he is surfing 2 foot gravely waves on an on Shore Day at their favorite break.

In the Hindu religion, a Brahman is the one supreme spirit in many forms experiencing itself. It is basically like God shattered himself or herself into 1 billion pieces and we are all that living embodiment of God or a peace of God experiencing itself subjectively. According to the Hindu religion, enlightenment is just realizing that you are Brahman. But the conundrum of understanding that you are Brahman is that you cannot say that you understand that you are Brahman otherwise you are not.

"A monk walked up to a hotdog vendor and ordered a hotdog. When asked what he wanted on his hotdog, he said "just make me one with everything."

A Brahman would be one with everything. Understanding it means not being able to explain it, and understanding that, means understanding that you are not supposed to even try to explain it. It's a bit of a paradox even to have to be able to explain it like I just did.

When talking with gurus, they usually claim to have found their enlightenment during some form of meditation. And they usually can't explain it, except for insulting it with our limited vocabulary of speech. All religions who have some type of enlightenment, agree that it has to be felt. It has to be experienced. It's not something that you can use words to explain.

So if words are the way humans understand things in most circumstances, how is it that we understand things that cannot be explained by words? Perhaps it has to be felt?

There's an old saying in the surfing world "Only a surfer knows the feeling." How does one describe what heaven sees? Can the feeling of being in love be put into words? Can you really describe what goes on inside of your body when you stare at a Sunset?

The beach boys had a song called "Catch a wave in your sitting on top of the World" I'm not sure if any of the Beach boys actually even surfed, but whoever was writing the songs was getting pretty close to how it actually feels to be an ocean dweller. Unfortunately it's been portrayed by Hollywood and most "posers" or "Barneys" As a sport for people who don't shave yet, that sit in their hippie van and smoke weed. But the truth behind the veil is stranger than fiction and more unbelievable than even I could imagine.

I know people that I've given up everything in their entire lives and lived on the beach and we're perfectly happy. In fact, very few times in my life have I met people that are dedicated surfers, that suffer from depression. It could be all that sunlight, meditation, reward systems, for the combination of all together. But one thing stands for certain, whatever we're doing we're doing right.

It doesn't take a scoreboard to tell us how good we're doing, even though the sports of competition surfing are quite amusing and fun to watch. But your average surfer doesn't need that scoreboard. We don't need $1 million to make us feel fulfilled, or a supermodel girlfriend or boyfriend to keep us completely stoked. It's as simple as catching the proper wave on the right day, it's like winning the lottery on a daily basis.

At the end of my life I don't think I'm going to think about all the times that I've worked, all the hearts that I've broken or the times I've had mine shattered. I think at the end of the day, when I'm in the twilight of my life feeding into the darkness, I'm going to look back and truly state the words I chose for the title of this book, "at least I surfed".

And for people stuck in-land, and all the land dwellers who have never even seen the ocean, I could not even imagine what it must be like to always chase money, significant others, material objects, or some type of status in society to fill your soul. I would imagine in some cases that the monks living a simple life in the mountains of Tibet might feel the same way about the rest of the world.

The only difference to me is that with surfing, it takes a lot of discipline just like a monk with discipline, but comes with a heavenly reward in the flesh. The biggest difference is the results right away. I have meditated for hours on end for years, and never reached any type of functional bliss. I have definitely reached bliss with meditation, I have definitely reached psychedelic states of mind, but never something so tangible and intangible at the same time as riding a wave.

I went to an ashram one time in Sedona Arizona and dropped a bunch of LSD. I was with some hippies that I knew from Northern California. I meditated next to a statue of Buddha for about 30 minutes before bursting into laughter. I've read a lot about Buddhism and found that most of it is a religion that's trying not to be a religion. Siddhartha was the original Buddha that was trying to steer clear of all the temples and worldly things that get wrapped up in religion.

His temple became the world, it was a language that he learned from the universe that surrounded him and made him feel one with everything. Almost as if he was talking to Himself the entire time. In the book Siddhartha, he finally finds peace next to a river and stays there the rest of his life just listening to the water flow.

To me this might be the greatest example of illuminating worldly temples and finding enlightenment within nature. And better yet, within water and the flow of life. While under LSD, watching those people meditate around a statue of somebody who did not want to be worshiped, my laughter became almost embarrassing. I removed myself from the situation, only to wander my way to the other side of Sedona to a place called Cathedral Rock. There was a Tuesday group of people that would set speakers in a circle and have an ecstatic dance.

I'll admit I was tripping pretty hard, but it made so much sense to me in that state of mind to just dance with those people. In ecstatic dance, people dance for about an hour without talking to each other, there is no judgment, only smiles in your own room of the universe to do as you please as long as you're doing no harm. I see people do headstands, I see people do breakdance moves, I've seen people just stand and rock back-and-forth with a smile on their face.

That's where I found, in my trip, that it seems to me that meditation while sitting still and closing your eyes seems to be a form of practicing for death. While on the other hand, this ecstatic dance was like a meditation in motion, and this meditation in motion invited life.

Surfing to me would be the ultimate form of meditation in motion. The best waves I've ever surfed, I felt like I was out of my body and someone else was surfing. Some call it being in the zone, but for me it was so much more than that, so much so that words insult it just like being a Brahman....or trying to describe enlightenment.

I don't think that your average Joe that decides after watching the movie "Point break" (which is actually a movie about enlightenment, written by a Buddhist) that he's going to become a surfer, ever has the thought of becoming some type of enlightened being by simply dropping 900 bucks on a board and going to the beach. But it happens. They say that it takes 80 years to achieve enlightenment in Tibet, my mentor in surfing used to tell me that it takes the average surfer at least four years of consistent dedication to become an actual surfer. I found this to be entirely true.

Four years of learning how to paddle, learning how to stand up, where the waves come from and why, and which angles the swells come in, and how to surf the waves properly without falling, and to do it with style. Four years to reach enlightenment. Four years to "accidental enlightenment".

Once you reach the enlightenment that I speak of that cannot be described in the words of the human language, what's next? For me, it was chasing the feeling. They say that a drug addict gets hooked on his first high and chases the dragon of that for the rest of his life. For most surfers it's the same, of course with us you can pull a Pat O'Connell and continuously get the best wave of your life.

The more skilled and better you get at the practice, the higher you become. So instead of chasing it like a drug addict who only gets it once and chases the good one the rest of his life, a surfer can continuously chase a better one, and that's what keeps us coming back.

CHAPTER 22

In India they would call it the law of karma. Some believe karma to be whatever you are doing this life reflects in the next. And some people believe that what you do in this life reflects in this life as well. In the Christian Bible, it says that you reap what you sow. In modern day, the saying is what goes around comes around. In essence, you basically get whatever you put into whatever it is you are doing or trying to accomplish.

If you want to be just a regular Saturday /Sunday weekend warrior surfer at your local break, just keep doing that. Show up every weekend, as the sun is rising and sip coffee with the old-timers who talk about how the waves used to be better. There's a novelty to that, in fact the people that taught me how to surf were all above 40 and they used to haze my ass every weekend. They made me earn it, every wave I took I had to earn. But eventually I ended up earning my spot in multiple line-ups.

The only way to earn your spot in the lineup is to constantly beat on your craft while not getting in the way. I've earned my spot in a couple of localized lineups over the years. Usually through staying the hell out of the way and catching a couple black eyes from some of the Bulldogs in the lineup. But you have to keep showing up and take the licks in order to earn it. It's the only way.

To be a ripper, you have to put in the time. When I first learned how to surf, I would take the bus to the beach at 7 AM, I'd stay at the Huntington Beach pier all day getting hassled by the locals, cut off and cut off by all the veterans, sometimes only catching one or two waves throughout the whole day as I got back on the bus at 6 PM and rode the hour back home. I had no idea I was putting my time in, and something was calling me to the ocean. But by the end of the first year I was as good as most of my friends who have been surfing their whole life as weekend warriors with their dad.

The only way to get barreled on a wave that's head high and come out, unless you are extraordinarily lucky, is to master the craft of barrel riding. They make it look so easy in the movies and the surf videos. But it is without a doubt one of the most hair-raising and frustrating things to learn. Mostly because in order to get a barreled you have to go to where the waves barrel. Also known as the danger zone.

"When the wave breaks here….don't be there." -Turtle "North shore"

To get barreled would be the ultimate in surfing. But to actually know how to ride a barrel consistently takes more than what meets the eye. You don't just show up, jump in the water, and drop into a barrel. You might look out during fall in Southern California at your local beach break and accidentally stumble upon one. But to fully get the experience where you've mastered it and know how to navigate through the barrel, over the foam ball, in the eye of the storm, you have to put your time in at a spot where it's consistent. To get that thrill where time slows down and you could almost see the molecules flying by your face...to fill the rush of when the time begins to speed back up as you come out, to see the light of day after you've been inside the eye of the storm, there's nothing much like it on this planet. But you have to put your time in.

I've listened to Allen Watts lectures on loop about enlightenment. His take is that it comes when you're not looking for it, and only after you have given up after a lifetime of trying. I take this as a very philosophical way of saying that it's more about letting go than trying to find it. Of course, without those years of searching, would you even have known what stumbled upon you when it does happen? Monks can spend years on monasteries, learning thousands of practices, only to find that what they were searching for was within.

I've often said that it takes the average surfer years to learn how to surf. That's in year one, you're just a wet cat, a buoy in the lineup that's getting in the way of everybody. You might catch some white water, and maybe even a reform on the inside, but that's not surfing. Then there's a year two, this is where you kinda understand what the lineup is all about. You somewhat know how to paddle into a wave, but you're still not out there on the big days, or shredding, or even paddling properly yet with your fetus arms. Year three you begin to gain a lot of strength, this is where you've earned your spot in the lineup, where you ride rail to rail surfing, and at this point you're starting to get comfortable and head high plus surf… maybe even developing a proper cutback. By year four you are looking for the biggest sets on the biggest days, you are relaxed in the water, you are pulling into the barrels, you are developing style.

You can tell how much time a guy puts into the water just by his style. If he's a stink bug, he's probably a Barney, which is somebody who only surfs every now and then claims to be the baddest surfer of all time. Then there's the super surfer, he most likely paddles into most of the waves and is a wave hog, yet rides with the sickest style, although he rips, people tend to yield to these people. Then there's the OG surfers that chill in the line-up as they usually have a "give a wave get a wave style."

But who is the super-surfer mastering the craft? Putting time in the water…and usually catching all the waves too. Is it because half the time they're jerks in the water? Perhaps, there is some type of cockiness one can get, once you put in the time and effort. Nothing different than a person who takes karate classes as opposed to somebody who trained with the Shaolin monk. There's gonna be a bit of ego that you have to have to make it to that level.

But with that ego comes a lot of experience and discipline. In order to get to a certain level, you have to put your ego to work. A lot of people who are in eastern philosophy believe that the ego is the enemy. I believe that the ego just needs something to do. And if you give it that something to do, you can harness the power of it.

To reap what you sow in the sport of kings, you really have to put your time in. You get what you put in, in the great law, that is the rules. So the next time you see a guy who rips, don't be jealous, be inspired. He definitely put his time in and so should you, just not at my surf break.

CHAPTER 23

Through all my research and discovery the only thing I can figure out is that I really don't know anything. I could spend most of my time studying history and reading about subjects and still not even touch the iceberg tip of knowledge. I have traveled far and wide and met people from many tribes, colors, and different walks of life only to find that we are all living in the same mystery.

I believe that there are certain things in life that no one will ever understand. I think life is designed that way. And indeed I do believe life was designed. I don't think it was a guy in the clouds with a beard. I think it's so far beyond complicated that our finite little minds could never grasp the concept.

Which God is correct? Is karma real? Is it from the slide for the last? Is Jesus really the only way? What about the rest of the world who never heard of him? These questions plague me in the research that I found confusing about religion.

I was never a very good student, but I could always go to the beach and jump in the water and feel good about myself. I could always get up at 4 AM, drive down to the beach, run across the freezing cold sand in January and dive into the ocean and it would change my entire existence for the day.

I see people go through rehab, AA, and have religious experiences. I see people crying at the altar, people surrendering their lives, and people giving up everything for God. I too have gone through a rehab of oceanic baptism, tried by fire while being caught on the inside, and surrendered to massive wipeouts.

I think that falling in love might be the closest thing I can use in a common human experience to describe the mystery of what I feel when the wind is slightly offshore and the waves are slightly overhead. I have been in love many times in my life, only to have my life come crashing down when it all ends. Unfortunately for us in life, it all ends anyway.

So what if you can fall in love every day? What if you could paddle out and make love to your mistress whenever you wanted? What if the rewards systems are designed to be like drugs where you have to get a hit on a constant basis in order to be fulfilled?

Some people find that void in life and fill it with all kinds of things, I personally like to fill it with the mystery of what makes me feel good about the ocean. To slide gently across that waters, to be in an environment that's calm and fierce all at the same time. To almost die every day, just to make yourself feel alive, is in itself something to be treasured in sacred bliss.

" What's so special about surfing?"

"Well.... What's so special about the wind? Surfing is to be with that mystery. To ride that mystery for as long as you can. And when it's over....that's cool.... because you know what? .... You were there! In line and on time."

-Matthew McConaughey-"Surfer Dude"

I've said it before, and I'll say it again, that life is nothing more than a massive mystery to all of us. It said that anybody that says otherwise I tried to convince you of something else, is trying to sell you something. Anybody that claims that they didn't have the answer, if you watch closely, well usually shortly after asking for money.

I'm not here claiming to know any answers. What I'm here to do is explain to you the answer that I found, for myself as an individual. and I make no claims to completely understand it. In fact this entire book was just trying to figure out why it was that I felt the way I do when I'm riding a wave in the ocean.

But with an understanding that I only have one life to live that I am aware of, the knowledge of knowing that one day the avatar that is Blake Butler, shall someday return back into ashes and dust.... is what leads me on my quest to find that mystery and to ride it as long as I can. And just like the surfer Dude quote above says "And when it's over, that's cool because you were there.

Most religious practices, yoga, meditation, or anything that people use to find peace in their lives, as in my observation, are just a way to stay in the present. Present becomes the past, so why not make a beautiful present. To me there's nothing better than the meditation in motion of curling up in the pocket or talking into a barrel as a form of staying in the present.

And one of the hardest things one can do is try to explain what it's like to feel the way that we do when all our reward systems are firing off in our heads, our muscles are satisfied with the shoulder burn, and Our mind is at peace. So many people have tried to sell you a peace of mind, and bastardized anything sacred, to the point where everything just sounds cliché.

To try and get your point across with something that's so personal makes you sound like some type of "wish they were" poet wannabe. I hear people talk about it with snowboarding, being in church, or meditating yourself into a Zen state of mind. I have tried all the above. Everything from skydiving to psychedelics. Everything from Tantric sex to bareknuckle boxing.

And I'm here to tell you that there's nothing like it, there's nothing like being in the ocean and catching the wave of the day.

And what's even more amazing about it, is the mysteriousness of what makes it all possible. I would say the mystery flavor is definitely my favorite flavor. I will never pretend to understand life, people, or what it is that we're here to do. But living my personal legend, while my soul is stuck in this body on this planet, surfing seems to be the only thing that makes sense.

Surfing really is to ride that mystery for as long as you can just like riding out life as long as you can. It's a mysterious dance with what I can identify as God. Not some guy in the sky with a beard, not somebody looking down, not even somebody. To me, God is that mystery. My religion is chasing that flow State, that mystery as long as I can.

CHAPTER 24

I can truly say that surfing saved my life. Not in the way that Jesus saves peoples lives. But in a real sense of keeping me out of trouble and occupying my time.

There was an old experiment done on rats with cocaine in the 1970s and 80s. They would get the rats addicted to cocaine and then give them two buttons to choose from. One button gave them food and water, the other, gave them another hit of cocaine.

Scientists were in disbelief at the fact that the rats, when addicted to cocaine, would keep hitting the button for it until they eventually died of starvation. This experiment became super famous and people talked about it for years.

There was another scientist however, who decided that the information was based on the environment in which they had kept the rats. If you had a choice between food and water, and cocaine when you were locked in a box, you would always choose the cocaine. The next scientist decided to do something different. This scientist decided that the animals were only choosing the drugs because there was no point to their life. They were not having fun.

During this scientist's experiment, the rats were given playgrounds, access to each other, and toys. During this experiment, the rats would almost never touch the cocaine buttons. They would in fact only choose food and water in between play sessions and visiting with their friends.

The difference in the experiment was the fact that the rats had some type of purpose besides sitting in a box. They had a fellowship, they had something to do. That's the difference when it comes to rats or people. Having a life's purpose is crucial to both your mental and physical health and to your sense of survival.

This same experiment can be said about myself and the people I grew up with. I have friends that Have never left a little town in Arizona that I got away from. Almost every single one of them are into some type of drug abuse. Almost every single one of them are either in jail, on drugs, or dead.

They, just like the rats, never left the box and subjugated themselves instead of pressing that cocaine button. To them, that's what life was. A series of moments of getting high and low. They had no knowledge outside of the little world that they created for themselves. And all the people that I know that have the same problems such as drugs and alcohol including myself, like when I found myself in the pit of despair of addiction, only when I had nothing else to do and nowhere else to be.

During the first half of 2018 while sitting on my father's deathbed, I drink myself stupid. My hands began to shake and my body began to sweat after a few months of it. I was locked in a box with nothing to do and nowhere to go. No matter how many little hobbies I picked up, nothing compared to surfing.

I was that rat in the experiment. When I wasn't given the proper playground to express myself, I fell deep into addiction and dependence. I'm not preaching about drugs or alcohol, in fact they are not that bad when given the correct circumstances, just like the rat experiment. What I'm preaching about is having something to live for. Having something for self-expression is one of the most important things a human can do for ourselves.

One of the only things that pulled me out of the depression, dependence, and addiction, was being able to figure out a way back to the ocean during the time with him. The most interesting experiment of my life was in my observations of what happens to people during stressing in a box like I was. I myself went crazy, I watched my whole world fold it on itself.

But just like the rats that were given a sense of purpose and self-expression, my whole life surfing is what did this for me. I smoked weed and drank just like every high school kid does. The difference for me, was I went home around 9 or 10 PM from the party. In the morning I got up and went for a surf while everybody else nursed a hangover with "The hair of the dog"

Anytime my boredom got the best of me I would jump in my car and go to the beach. It was my playground and my sense of purpose. Instead of seeing what the kids were doing while smoking cigarettes in the alley across town, I was at the beach, even when the waves weren't that good.

While talking to an elderly gentleman one time, I asked him what the secret of life was, he responded "You got to have something to live for." I took that to heart. Along with that and reading the experiments on the rats, not to mention watching myself go into the lockdown mode and the hysteria I had created for myself, I believe that surfing really did save my life. It definitely saved my sanity.

Every time I took a quick trip to California to catch some waves, it was like an instant quick fix. All my depression, self-doubt, anything negative that was going on my mind would just disappear. It was my fix.

Sitting with my father on his deathbed is something I will never regret, but it was definitely something that made me go crazy. I sat in a room with him for nine months, watched him die slowly, and then dealt with the repercussions of my drinking habits that developed in that box, mixed with the sense of not having a life's purpose.

There was nothing easy about the lockdown of hospice, of course it was followed up by another type of lock down. When he passed away September 2019, I had no idea what the world was in store for. Even surfing became illegal. I was in a lockdown for a whole year before the real lockdowns began and my insanity had its chance to stretch its legs.

CHAPTER 25

I had been sitting in Arizona for way too long. I had done my Sun Dance. My rights of passage with my father and his death were more than a Sundance to me. I had been tried by fire and made it out while seeing him off to the other-side.

I was still on this side, and in order to heal, I could not sit still. I needed to flow.

I called Keith and he sent me a plane ticket on the passes to LA. My grieving was silent because I knew that my father wanted to go. Cancer has a way of making you want to die. And by the time you do it, you already look dead.

My grieving was more of a selfish one. However, I already knew the cure. Waves. And for this depression, lots of waves. To celebrate his life, I knew I had to live mine to the fullest. I surfed Palos Verdes and Huntington Beach for a month straight just trying to get my arms in shape and get my head in the right place. Keith had a job for me to go up and down the coast moving an apartment building for him with a couple U-Haul trucks full to the brim.

Every time I went to Humboldt, I would get a couple waves while I was there, and then I would fly to LA and get a couple waves in between the truck hauling. I was making money, getting waves, and getting ready for my next Peruvian excursion. Hopefully nothing happens this time. After all, it would be my fifth attempt to make it to South America and into the land of the endless lefts.

As I began to make arrangements for my trip to South America, I kept hearing about a virus on the news in China. It seemed like a pretty big deal on every station in January 2020. I was beginning to make my moves within the next week or two to hop a plane to South America, but something didn't feel right.

When you're in your flow state, what you begin to notice is that sometimes you get pulled in a direction. Sometimes that direction doesn't make any sense whatsoever. Sometimes you're trying to zig when it wants you to zag. Unfortunately for this lifestyle there is no manual, and most teachers will agree that it is a personal journey and your truth is your truth.

I didn't fill the pull to South America for some reason, I had the ticket again, I had people waiting for me there, but something just didn't feel right. I started to get a pull back to Arizona. It made entirely no sense to me. That was the last place I wanted to be. No waves to be found in the desert. But when you're in a certain state of mind, you just have to have the faith that you're being pulled in the right direction.

I skipped Humboldt on a bus and did not explain anything to anybody. I did not know how I was gonna get home, but I just kept feeling something pull me south. When I got to San Francisco I stayed with a friend named Rhea that I had met at Burning man. She told me she wanted to gift me her car. All proof that the flow was correct. I wasn't sure how I was getting home and now I had a car out of nowhere.

Her husband Josh was quite the avid surfer himself. He lent me a board and a suit in the morning and we got some waves at ocean beach, situated directly across the street from their place. After the surf I kept feeling the pull south.

I made it to Arizona to help fix up my father's house to get ready to sell. Within a month, it was all over the news. COVID-19 had entered the United States and was spreading like wildfire. In my mind, I felt a little bit protected. I don't think I would've been able to post up just about anywhere during this lockdown or pandemic.

My flow knew that all the flow was going to stop. The universe seems to know that the best place for me during this pandemic was to be landlocked in Arizona. In fact I kept seeing surfers getting arrested for going to the beach on the television. Nobody was even allowed out of their house to the point where LA looked like a ghost town.

Now here, posted up in the middle of the desert just north of Phoenix, up in the mountains, I'm landlocked but still in my flow. Nobody knew how long this pandemic was going to last but it gave me time to sit down, collect my thoughts, grieve properly, and put my thoughts in this book. Sometimes being landlocked is useful.

Of course, you know I had to figure out a way to surf. Even during the pandemic I had bought a minivan. I used it to quietly drive the six hours to the coast during the middle of the week or anytime the swell is good and grab a surf. I threw a board in the back, and made it seem a little homely. Even though in the last couple of years during this pandemic I might only surf twice to three times a month, it's still top priority in my life.

I feel that the pandemic was a way to stop the flow of the entire planet. Everybody locked themselves inside of their house and followed whatever the TV said like George Orwell had predicted in his books so long ago. Usually when you dam up water, it builds pressure. For me, it made me break a lot of bad habits and gave me time to think. This pandemic gave me time to write out this book.

I am however using my time in a productive way in many different avenues. For instance, the second this pandemic is finished, I will have been planning a trip to Peru for some time now. Looking like the universe made me extra hungry to go. You can bet if we are ever able to travel again, I'll finally make it to the land of lefts and "worship" my God from a corner pocket of Chicama.

I can't say that I actually worship anything, but I can say that I live the lifestyle based on a belief. That belief is just a flow state. Just one thing connecting to another, that eventually connects to everything. Perhaps it's all in my mind, but it's a very real subject that all enlightened beings have talked about, and it's something that's real to me.

To proclaim this action in motion as a religion may be a bold statement, but it's the closest thing to what some people call God that I can conceive. To live in the moment, to be happy for no reason, to have fun without any rules, to flow, in life and on water is a beautiful way to live.

I've grown comfortable with living in Arizona and just surfing a few times a month. It seems like the older I get, the less I need to do it every day. I mostly just go when the waves are good, like a spoiled kid. I still fly to Hawaii during the winter and get my surf in tropical waters when it's cold on the mainland. I can't see a future where this lifestyle is not top priority.

I do know one thing, if I'm ever feeling short with people, grumpy out of nowhere, or like I'm losing my mind, I know exactly what it is I have to do. I hop in my little minivan and I cruise to the coast, these days I don't even tell anybody else, I roll up and I see my mistress ... the ocean.

I paddle out full of thankfulness with no intentions but to flow and dance on the canvas of God's playground. I now live my life in a flow state that can only be found when you let go, when you climb out of your mind and into the moment. Life is just a series of moments until it stops. When mine stops, the only thoughts that I could fathom going through it in that last second on that last breath....

...At least I surfed.

FINAL THOUGHTS

Through all of my research, through all of my experiences, the religion of surfing is what I based my faith in. I just like all religions of the world, it's going to be controversial. To me it's just that it's very personal.

When I meet somebody who has surfed for many years, there is a piece within their eyes I can only hope to find in the temples of Krishna, Jesus, and Buddha. When I paddle out by myself, it's just me and the universe, dancing through this thing I call life. It's joy at its purest.

Most religions are from ancient days. They tell stories of experiences of people you have never met, and places most people have never been, in times that people will never understand. Surfing allows you to live in the moment, at a time that is yours, in a place that you are home. The only understanding that you have to develop is your own.

The art of sliding across water, in a flow state, while having an outer body experience is the bliss that I find in my heart that doesn't have to make sense to anybody else. Spirituality is when you believe in your own hallucinations, religion is when you believe in a different person's hallucinations. I believe in mine and I encourage you to have your own.

There is an experience waiting for you out there, whether it be sliding across water at your local break, or just going with the flow of life and riding it like a wave, it's entirely up to you. I definitely encourage everybody to try something that's out of your element, and become entirely enveloped in it. Through taking the leap of faith, and living in a flow state, I hope that one day you too can have a religious experience.

Just like all sages and mystics, there has been passed down wisdom through all bases of faith. In the Bible it was the 10 Commandments of life, and in the back of this book, I'll bring you the 10 Commandments of surfing. I hope that you can follow and abide by the guidelines that I have learned as an ocean dwelling bringer of wisdom.

THE 10 COMMANDMENTS OF SURFING

1. There is only one ocean. Respect the ocean and do not pollute.

2. Respect all who dwell in the ocean both sea creatures and tourists

3. Give a wave get a wave

4. Dial shall not covet thy neighbor's wave

5. Make time for a pilgrimage to the motherland Hawaii. Respect the locals.

6. Teach the groms respect your elders

7. Do not lie about your ride do not make false claims

8. Honor all wave riders no matter what they ride

9. Don't be a kook

10. Thou shall Have fun and enjoy the ride

1. There is only one ocean. Respect the ocean, and do not pollute.

There is enough to say about Southern California after a good rain. Or any inner city for that matter when it comes to the pollution that humans cause on our playground in the ocean. I remember seeing a picture on Instagram that a pro surfer had put up, it showed a man getting shacked out of his mind with the lip of the wave almost full of trash. The world was up in arms about the photograph, but nobody seemed to do anything about it.

You don't have to be part of the Sea Shepherd's (which is an awesome organization that's cleaning up our oceans in a massive way) To contribute to the cleanup of our sacred waters. There's something as simple as every time you surf on your way back to the car, pick up some trash from the beach, or how about not throwing stuff in the sand to begin with. One of the best things we could do is teach the groms and Younger generation about the effect it has when you either clean up or when you pollute.

One single person is never going to stop giant corporations from drilling and spilling. But what we can do is an individual change and with enough individuals, it can become a collective that changes and cleans up to sea. But the first step to the equation is just not thrashing it in the first place.

The first rule of changing something is to change yourself. You have to be the change you want to see and set examples. If the ocean is going to get cleaned up and stay clean, we have to start with ourselves and our own carbon footprint. So the next time you're out enjoying a surf in the beautiful ocean, on your way back to the car just grab a piece of trash every single day, and if you surf 200 times a year that's 200 pieces of trash that you removed from the ocean for your wave karma.

2. Respect all who dwell in the ocean, sea creatures and tourists.

Let's face it, we get a little bit spoiled nine months out of the year when the water gets cold in most places for winter. It's a different story when you live in Hawaii and the weather is on a simmer in a constant endless summer. But in any case, surfers are not the only people or things in the water.

There comes a time for every surfer when they begin surfing and they are kind of like a buoy in the water. And even before that, when they were just children or tourists playing in the Shorebreak getting in the way of every Surfer. Those that are experts always forget about their beginnings. Most beginnings are humbling.

But let's not forget about the days when we were eating sand and building Sandcastles. Let's not forget about the days when we discovered the ocean and fell in love. Let us not forget about the days that we decided that the ocean was going to be our mistress and that we would never neglect her again.

The ocean is big enough for all of us, there's always another wave, there's always another day. Let us share this beautiful playground with her all winter. Let us also remember that we're not actually the locals no matter how close you live. Remember that the locals are actually sea life. Let us respect all those who dwell in the ocean.

3. Give a wave... to get a wave.

If you were to take every religion, every philosophy, and everything that you've ever learned within your life since the day you were born, you will come to the same conclusion that all the great philosophers and ascended masters have.... what goes around comes around. Some call it the Golden rule, but it's definitely one that is important and should be maintained on a regular basis.

Nobody likes a wave hog. I don't care how good you think you are, how cool you think you look, or how bad you shred. If you're walking all over people to get to it, you ain't nothing but a hog. If you get a good wave don't paddle out in a crowded line up and go straight back to the peak, give the next guy a chance, you have no idea what they're going through. If you were in a crowded lineup and you got the wave of the day, maybe go down the beach a little bit and let somebody else score.

This is a hard thing to learn if you are a weekend warrior at Huntington Beach pier. Or if you're trying to regulate in the lineup at Pipeline. Whoever you are, the Golden rule is called the Golden rule for a reason and it should be followed and respected. You never know when somebody else's last wave might be, so don't be a wave hog. If you get a good wave, give one back. It's all about sharing the stoke.

4. Thou shalt not covet thy neighbor's wave.

This one goes for every surfer who's ever been in a crowded lineup, or dropped in on anybody, which is everyone who ever lived and actually goes on a regular basis. It is not uncommon to drop in on somebody, apologize right away. Don't be that punk that gives you the cold shoulder after taking the wave of the day, pulling into the barrel directly in front of you. Always give the benefit of the doubt to the guy closest to the peak.

If you drop in on somebody's wave you might as well be flirting with their significant other right in front of them. There is nothing worse than a snake. And if you do miss the wave of the day and someone else grabs it, give them a hoot and holler, maybe a little Shaka. Don't be green with jealousy. Nobody likes that. Be inspired and enjoy your own wave.

5. Make time for a pilgrimage to Hawaii, respect the locals.

If you were Jewish, your pilgrimage would be Israel, if you were Muslim, it would be Mecca. But as a Surfer, our pilgrimage is to the motherland of surfing, Hawaii. Hawaii is the birthplace of surfing, it's actually up for debate between Peru and Hawaii historically, but surfing was first written about by Captain James Cook during the first exploration of the Hawaiian island chain.

Hawaii is definitely the land of the endless summer. With the temperature always on a simmer, the water clean and blue, and waves for all levels of surfing. It's aloha spirit lives on to this day through the indigenous Hawaiians that populate the area. And it's a true test of Surfer to make the pilgrimage to the motherland.

There is also the Dark Side of your pilgrimage which is surfing waves with open ocean speeds, dodging reefs and Vanna, and trying your best not to piss off the locals. So when your pilgrimage is made, the checklist would be to pay homage to the Hawaiian people. Surf Waikiki at least once in your life to really tap into the spirit of the original surfing way of life. Definitely try to push yourself to go into something a little bit bigger, heavier and deeper than you've ever pushed yourself before. If you want to surf the biggest wave of your life, I would suggest doing it there because the waves are close to perfect. Not to mention if you actually do wipe out and get into some trouble they have the best lifeguards on the planet.

The number one rule is if you go to Hawaii, and you want to experience the aloha spirit, you have to show it yourself. Remember to slow down. Remember that everything moves at half pace in Hawaii including the traffic and the people. So when you make your pilgrimage don't forget that it is somebody else's land that was taken on paper, but they still own it in spirit, they belong to it, not the other way around. So make sure you have at least one pilgrimage to the beautiful motherland of the lifestyle we all take part in, to pay respects to the locals.

6. Teach groms, respect your elders.

When I was a grom, I used to take the bus to the beach. There was an older guy down the street that would surf at 4 AM every day named Kelly. He saw me walking down the street with my surfboard coming from his neighborhood, he stopped and told me to meet him at his house at four in the morning tomorrow. I developed a relationship with this man that rivals any of my family. This guy was like the bear in big Wednesday. He taught me how to read weather maps, where the waves come from during which season, and most importantly how to ride waves with style.

Since he and I lost touch throughout time and he moved to the East Coast, I have been a surfing mentor for multiple surfers. It was sort of a "pay it forward" thing because that was one of the single most influential things that happened to me in my life. I believe that everybody in every aspect of life should have a mentor if they're going to do something good.

To this day when I see groms struggling in the water, I will do two things, make fun of them to their face the way all the older dudes used to Haze me in the water, And 2, straighten them up, and look out for them. The same goes for the older gentleman in the lineup. I've had to pull both children and elderly out of the water multiple times in my surfing career. I was pulled out by a couple locals at the wedge my first time when I was a grom, without them, I may not have made it. Unfortunately I've also pulled multiple elderly out of the water and some that did not make it. Such as the circle of life. When you're in the water, and you are a strapping young

Surfer, it is your duty to look out for the groms, As well as the elderly. And don't forget to respect all the uncles.

7. Do not lie or make false claims about your ride.

Surfers are pretty honest people.... except for when it comes to surfing. I have told my share of white lies, and false claims coming out of non-barrels. I don't know how many times my friend has told me that the waves were going off only to drive all the way to the beach and find 2 foot on-shore gravity waves and a lonely friend that didn't want to surf alone. Those are usually the same friends that go on surf trips and claim to score the entire time. But every time you seem to go with that same guy, you never score but his stories are outrageous.

If we're talking about the size of a wave, the rule of thumb is to always under sell it. We all have that one friend who claims to be surfing 10 foot waves on a day-to-day basis. 10 foot waves are a very serious thing and I only know a handful of people personally that actually take on 10 foot waves. I can count in my lifetime maybe 20 sessions where I saw a 10 ft wave. The rule of thumb is that if you think it's 10 feet just tell your friend it was six. Because if it really was 10 foot, they would already know.

8. Honor all wave riders no matter what they ride.

Some people can get a little bit cocky about being a short border at their local break and the number one ripper in the area. But nobody really likes that guy. And nobody really likes the guy who cuts off the body borders, yells at the tourists, or long borders.

The truth of the matter is we're all just trying to get waves. Everyone of us came to play with nature and there's always plenty to go around. So the next time you see somebody with some new wave riding apparatus, tip your hat and see how it goes because you never know when the next bodyboard or hydrofoil is gonna come.

9. Don't be a kook.

When it comes to the ultimate Surfer, what matters is that you can ride any wave on any board in any condition and do it well with style. The kook is not so much a beginner according to this commandment. A kook is somebody who knows the rules and chooses not to follow them. A kook as someone who shows up to a new brake and tries to take over.

Some people define a kook as somebody who drags their leash on the way up the beach, or somebody who wears their wetsuit for hours after they've been out of the water. Sometimes it's even in the way you wear your shorts or what for the ride. But a real kook is somebody who's just out to ruin somebody else's time.

A real kook is somebody who doesn't respect the locals, doesn't respect the tourists, doesn't respect the ocean, and doesn't respect themselves. Don't get me wrong, there's definitely kooks that have funky Styles that can stink up the place but that's a completely different type of Kook.

The kook that this commandment commands you not to be is the one that acts like he's better than any Surfer in the water. The one that paddles around a kid to cut off an old man, to get the wave of the day. Don't be a kook.

10. Thou shall have fun and enjoy the ride.

In retrospect life itself is just one giant wave and when it crashes we all end up back in the ocean. In Costa Rica they have a saying called Pura Vida, which means pure life. This basically means that I got one life and so do you and let's just help each other out and not ruin it for each other.

You never know when your last ride is going to be, or if you have 1 million more coming. The ultimate commandment is also the best advice, have fun no matter what you do in life, always have a good time because even if it turns out to be a bummer, at least you had fun. So go travel, talk to strangers, meet people from around the world that are chasing the same waves you are. Doing this, you can relate on a level that no one else can.

Always dream of that trip to Bali? Sounds fun doesn't it? You might have 80 summers, 80 winters, 80 Springs, and 80 falls, but you need to fit it in there before those are up. Don't take it too seriously, just like anything else in life. Have fun. Remember that there are two different types of people on a roller coaster and the same goes for life, The one who screams and holds on, or the one that hoots and hollers and puts their hands up and enjoys the ride.
My best advice is to be the one having the most fun. That's a command.
Amen.

Made in the USA
Monee, IL
31 July 2023